cover: @photo by Stephan Vanfleteren

www.disvoir.com
www.facebook.com/groups/disvoir/

ISBN 978-2-914-563-92-5

PRINTED IN EUROPE

LEE CHANG DONG

LEE CHANG DONG

JEAN-PHILIPPE CAZIER

VÉRONIQUE BERGEN

ANTOINE COPPOLA

translated from French by
VALENTINE LEYS

◀ 1

2 ▶

THE SECRET BODY OF CINEMA

THE BODY AS A SENSORIAL FRAMEWORK OF PHYSICAL, SOCIAL, POLITICAL AND NATURAL REALITY

A frontal shot of a flat surface, and smoke. This is *Burning*'s opening image: an abstract, intriguing shot, which does not simply denote absence - that of a character for example - but absence within the image. Something is there, it seems to be and must be there, it should be there, but it is not visible in the image. Something should be present but it is not visible; it is not present within a setting that is designed to show and even exhibit: the image. It is this absence within the image that the image constructs and signals: if there is no smoke without fire, then there can be no cigarette smoke without someone who has lit this cigarette and is smoking it. What is missing from this image is the cause of the smoke: the smoker, their body and their body's visibility. To quote Gilles Deleuze, we could say that the breach of the sensory-motor schema that opens this filmic moment no longer affects solely the incapacitated body, or the body that takes on aberrant forms, but affects the action itself, i.e. the phenomenon, the event. Without a mouth to expel it, without a smoker, the cigarette smoke exists for itself as an aberration within an aberrant world, a ghostly vision suggesting the invisible, at the center of an image as elusive as this smoke. This cinematographic image resonates with Francis Bacon's paintings.

The invisible of the image

If Lee Chang-dong's films feature facts or events whose cause is explicit and rationally conceivable – in *Secret Sunshine*, the woman goes insane *because* her child has been murdered; in *Poetry*, the grandmother has a sexual intercourse *in order to* get the money she needs –, they also show images whose cause or rational context is absent. In *Oasis*, a baby elephant suddenly appears in the apartment, and the characters start dancing to music that has nothing to do with the music we had heard a second earlier, when these same characters were stuck in a traffic jam... This mechanism is pushed to an extreme in *Burning*: everything is geared towards the destruction of rational links, of the certainty of causal relations, of rational explanations. *Burning* exposes the viewer to a world that is alien: an irrational, meaningless and unthinkable world, a world that cannot be reduced to the usual categories of our relation to the world, to the modalities, means and purposes of this relation. A world that we cannot control and which can only be contemplated through its strange and mysterious visibility. A world, therefore, that escapes both knowledge and power and whose existence for us is a matter of belief.

Looking at this more slowly: we only identify cigarette smoke as such after a few seconds, and from this we only deduce the primary absence of the smoker's body only after first perceiving an image that we do not understand, that we cannot spontaneously identify or decipher. In the very first moments, this image is incomprehensible, unrecognizable. It is only after the fact that we perceive it as having a meaning and potentially relating to a story (a man smokes a cigarette...), and that we can integrate it into our common perceptual and mental universe (in *Oasis*, the opening image first appears visually and sonically independent, and can only be identified much later in the film as an image of the girl's room; conversely, in *Poetry*, it is the final image, which draws a parallel between the grandmother and the young suicide victim, that appears independent and incomprehensible : the analogy between the two characters is not entirely rationalizable, especially since the girl we then see on screen, truly «present», visible, staring at the camera and smiling faintly, has been dead since the beginning of the film...). The opening image in *Burning* also eludes the conditions of representation: not through the absence of an image but by placing absence at the heart of the image – a visibility that contains some invisible, an image that escapes the rules of image by avoiding the obvious and the visible. In other words, an imageless image, which we cannot recognize, think or perceive comprehensively...

The image-body of cinema

This opening image is articulated around the body, it starts from the body, and more precisely - and paradoxically - from its very absence. In this respect, it could be seen as a defining image for *Burning*, where absent bodies proliferate (the cat, the girl, a piece of fruit, the burnt barns, etc.) but also for Lee Chang-dong's cinema in general: a cinema of the body, or better, a cinema of the body in cinema. The point is not simply to make images of the body, as if the body existed independently of the image that shows it, and if image was only a neutral means of display. Bachelard has shown that in science, observation and measuring instruments are not neutral but that they condition both observation and the thing observed: we see what the instruments allow us to see, according to the modalities they create. A scientific phenomenon is a function of an instrument. The same may apply to the body in film: the cinematographic body is not captured intact from the world, but it is the product of what film can grasp of the body and what it can do to the body. Lee Chang-dong tends to film what cinema and cinematographic image can do to the body, what happens to the body through cinema: the production of an image-body, a filmic body, resonating with unprecedented possibilities that can perhaps only exist on film. Lee Chang-dong thus questions the body from the perspective of film, of cinematographic image, of what the body becomes *with* film. What we see on screen is not «the body» but an image-body, with all the possibilities created by the body's cinematographic nature.

A key approach for Lee Chang-dong seems to consist in questioning the presence of the body – the body as a necessary presence – by challenging what appears as the primary characteristic of this presence: the body's visibility. This questioning of the body is a key issue in Lee Chang-dong's cinema, and it forms part of a broader investigation of visibility and presence – for which the body provides a privileged medium. Through this questioning, Lee Chang-dong creates becomings of the body that in turn affect everything that is connected to the body and entailed by the body: incorporeality, immateriality, mind, relation to the world, drive, visibility, presence, absence, desire, perception, affect... The questioning of the body as present and visible is in fact characteristic of cinema: this presence and visibility are by definition paradoxical since the body in film is first and foremost the image - and sound - of a body; or better yet, it is an image-body whose bizarre existence requires to some extent the body's dematerialization, its evanescence. Cinema creates ghosts, spectral bodies, metamorphic bodies – bodies that are simultaneously present and absent.

Image and thought

Going back to *Burning*'s first image, we see that it eradicates the usual logic of relations. What should be visible - the body - to give coherence and meaning to the scene, is not, and this invisibility of the cause of what we see prevents us from understanding what we see and from seeing it completely. The fact is not intelligible because the conditions for its intelligibility - the context, the determination of the cause - are not met. Separating the effect from its cause, removing the body and its action from the visible, contributes to producing an image that escapes common rationality and the causal relationship that is necessary for our understanding not only of the image, but also of the world in general. *Burning* is built on the systematic erasure of the rational determination of causes, on cinematographic gestures (shots, script, narrative, etc.) that blur the context, make it ambiguous, obscure, plural, undecidable. In other words, this image – the few seconds that it lasts – implies the eradication of a totality that would make it recognizable and intelligible. The image excludes what we usually expect, the condition of thinking, of meaning, of identification, of recognition – that is, of

3 ▶

representation: it excludes totality, which remains indeterminate, vague and open. This absence of a totality that would encompass and unify what we see and think runs throughout *Burning*. This is what makes it a particularly exciting and important film that eludes the spectacle of image as well as the meaning of the narrative: a film inhabited by something beyond, which constantly slips away and remains invisible, which worries and obscures the thought. A film that in itself becomes a forever open and mobile thought, body and world.

On another level, this means that meaning and understanding are only possible within a given framework. Rationality requires the existence and creation of a specific context of rationalization that encompasses and unifies reality. This truth, long stated by the epistemology of science, first revealed by Kantian philosophy and repeated in more or less radical forms by all philosophy after Kant, is turned by Lee Chang-dong into a cinematographic principle as well as into a principle that presides over the relation to the world and to the self. Lee Chang-dong's cinema is based on this truth and on the relativity of the frames of reference that it can imply. It aims to disrupt the context and the frame, with films whose very purpose is to erase the frame and to reveal the impossibility of totality, whose context is in constant motion, removing the possibility of rationalization, understanding and perception – and therefore, of possession and control. Understanding, recognizing or mastering no longer matter: the film imposes on us a passion that affects the body and mind, the world and our relationship to the world, that impacts who we are in front of the film and who we can no longer be. The body and the mind discover what they also are, and that which we are not usually able to experience clearly: the paradoxical power of being affected and radically lost, of no longer being able to think or insert ourselves into sensory-motor patterns. This passivity is not negative: it is the condition of another way of thinking, of another world, of another body – the condition of de-alienation, which is perhaps what art can achieve, and concerns aesthetics as much as ontology and thought. *Burning* produces this conversion and replaces action by contemplation, thought by the wandering of thought, knowledge by belief – it replaces the world by its absence: that is, by a liberating disorder.

The cinema of the out-of-frame

Lee Chang-dong's characters often find themselves caught up in environments and settings to which they do not belong, which they pass through without recognizing or understanding them and from which they are rejected. They experience these environments and what constitutes them but also the disarticulation of these environments, the logical and social frameworks that prevail in them, introducing what will produce an erasure of the framework, an inefficiency of necessary codes and rules, a flight beyond its limits and conditions. Lee Chang-dong likes to use shaky camera, with the camera following a character's instability and movements, mostly because this process challenges the notion of frame and reflects the impossibility of capturing things in a precise and predefined frame. On the contrary, things appear to escape the frame and only surge in to better disappear. The shaky camera creates a sense of perpetual de-framing: the frame keeps disappearing and what is filmed remains out-of-frame, forever eluding the image and remaining beyond the realm of the visible, and beyond the visible's visibility. The purpose of this process is not to reflect a character's subjective point of view, or to immerse the viewer into what is shown. The shaky camera creates a moving world that keeps escaping its own boundaries and remains instable. Reality cannot be circumscribed into a totality: it remains fragmented, enigmatic and insoluble. In this cinema, the world understood as one disappears and the thought darkens. Our eyes close: not for sleeping but rather to see more acutely, overwhelmed by the invisible. Through this perpetually de-framed and unstable cinematographic frame, Lee Chang-dong creates the conditions for a permanent de-framing of the world. The things he films elude any fixed and pre-existing frame – the conditions for throwing thought and perception into a state of panic, always in relation to what remains off-frame, to what lies beyond thought, perception and the world. The unthinkable and the imperceptible prevail, in a world taken over by chaos. The world becomes a pure enigma, a sum of questions. The mind can only ask questions without possible answers, caught in a ceaseless experience of the undecidable, the unidentifiable, the meaningless, and the irrational.

In most cases, this feeling is experienced by Lee Chang-dong's characters because something occurs – an encounter, a corpse, a change of environment, a disappearance, etc. – and reverses what was known by making it problematic, redistributing established coordinates according to new, unassimilable configurations. As a filmmaker, Lee Chang-dong does not just illustrate this experience by representing it: he develops purely cinematographic means out of it and creates films that *are* this very experience – films that *are* the world that begins to exist when the dissemination of any framework is pushed to its limits in one possible direction. Hence the importance in Lee Chang-dong's work of the question of the frame - and first of all in the cinematographic sense of the

◀ 4

◀ 5

6 ▶

8 ▶▶

7 ▶

term - and its relation to what is out-of-frame, hence the importance of the question of what is on camera vs. off camera, and the connection or lack thereof between the two. Hence also the creation of narratives and of a narrative logic that include their own disruption, challenging and discontinuity as other divergent beginnings continue to emerge. The narrative sees the emergence of provisionally unifying and meaningful logics, that seem to allow for the definition of a whole, but are nonetheless denied, defeated, replaced by other provisional beginnings, other different and open logics. In Lee Chang-dong's cinema each narrative frame includes, in more or less obvious ways, a deframing movement that cancels and replaces it, and transforms it within another context of repetition and transformation. Lee Chang-dong favors this dynamic of narrative de-framing which affects characters, identities and spaces – as well as bodies which are, in his cinema, perhaps the central place of this perpetual movement of birth and death, of disappearance and appearance, of framing and de-framing. How can one film a body and the context in which this body can exist? How can the image make the body present, and how can the body reduce itself to this presence in and through the image? Is the visible body all that the body can be, or is visibility only one of the body's many possible modalities? Does the body necessarily imply presence? Countless questions arise, and Lee Chang-dong's cinema invents cinematographic means of asking them, of bringing them to life, of turning them into an aesthetic inhabited by the existence of other bodies – of other forms of the body but also of other forms of the world, other relationships to the world, other subjects or non-subjects, in a world that is constantly disappearing and being created.

One could say that Lee Chang-dong generalizes the principles of cut versus jump cut, by extending them beyond editing or beyond the continuity between shots. The wrong match becomes the law of the film and the law of the world, of being, of thinking, and of course of the body. While *Poetry* could appear as a more traditional film than *Burning*, a film that follows a coherent and simple narrative thread, it nevertheless includes a disruption of identities, a gap between what is supposed to be and what is. The film is drawn towards what is non-identifiable, alien, out-of-frame or towards the absence of totality, which deeply disrupts thought, redistributing everything that seemed to have been set up, recognized and thought, but without providing any new keys or allowing for the reconstruction of a coherent totality. The grandson, in line with the teenagers of his generation (school, television, computer, friends, etc.) eventually turns out to be a rapist or even, indirectly, a murderer. The grandmother, who lived an uneventful and conventional life, ends up selling her body. The young girl who had died at the beginning of the film nevertheless appears alive and smiling at the end, without any element making it possible to clearly connect this apparition with what came before it, disrupting the narrative thread and the film's apparently realistic nature as well as its so far linear temporality. The film ends without an explanation for what we have just seen, without giving us the means to understand it or to relate it to our habits, to what we «knew» as thought and the world. This coherent film embraces its own incoherence and leaves it open, cancelling the totality that we believed we had identified.

Secret Sunshine follows a similarly open-ended pattern: the school principal becomes a criminal without remorse; religion, which appeared as a ground for understanding and interpretation, becomes absurd; the new city, which offered the promise of a new life, becomes a nightmare; the conventional young woman, with her attachment to order, rules and rigor (she is a piano teacher), loses her mind; and the film ends on this madness, with a banal and meaningless sequence and shot which, far from closing the circle of a coherent, unifying totality, produces an open and endless film. Identities keep being reversed, the narrative is disrupted and time shifts: everything that seemed to fit within an obvious and recognized framework is denied by a disruption of logical links and of social, cultural, intellectual and aesthetic presumptions, as tenuous connections create a sense of incoherence – this term is of course used here in a positive sense – that pervades the entire film. The principle at work is that of incoherent juxtaposition, differentiality, missing connections. Lee Chang-dong's cinema values flaws, gaps, false connections and differences: it refuses the possibility of totalization as well as that of an encompassing and overhanging framework, while on the contrary asserting the truth of the fragment, of the relative, of the ephemeral, of mobility, of what remains open and thus by definition unrepresentable, absent and invisible. This openness circulates throughout Lee Chang-dong's films and informs *Burning* in its entirety.

Open bodies

Bodies are affected by the absence of totality, by this openness that pervades them and drives them out-of-frame, takes them out of themselves and makes them be something other than what they are. Bodies proliferate, multiply and become detached from any sense of identity: the domestic body becomes a prostituted body; the present body is an absent body; the wise body becomes host to uncontrollable madness; the regulated, normative body becomes the instrument of a crime; the dead body becomes

9 ▶

10 ▶

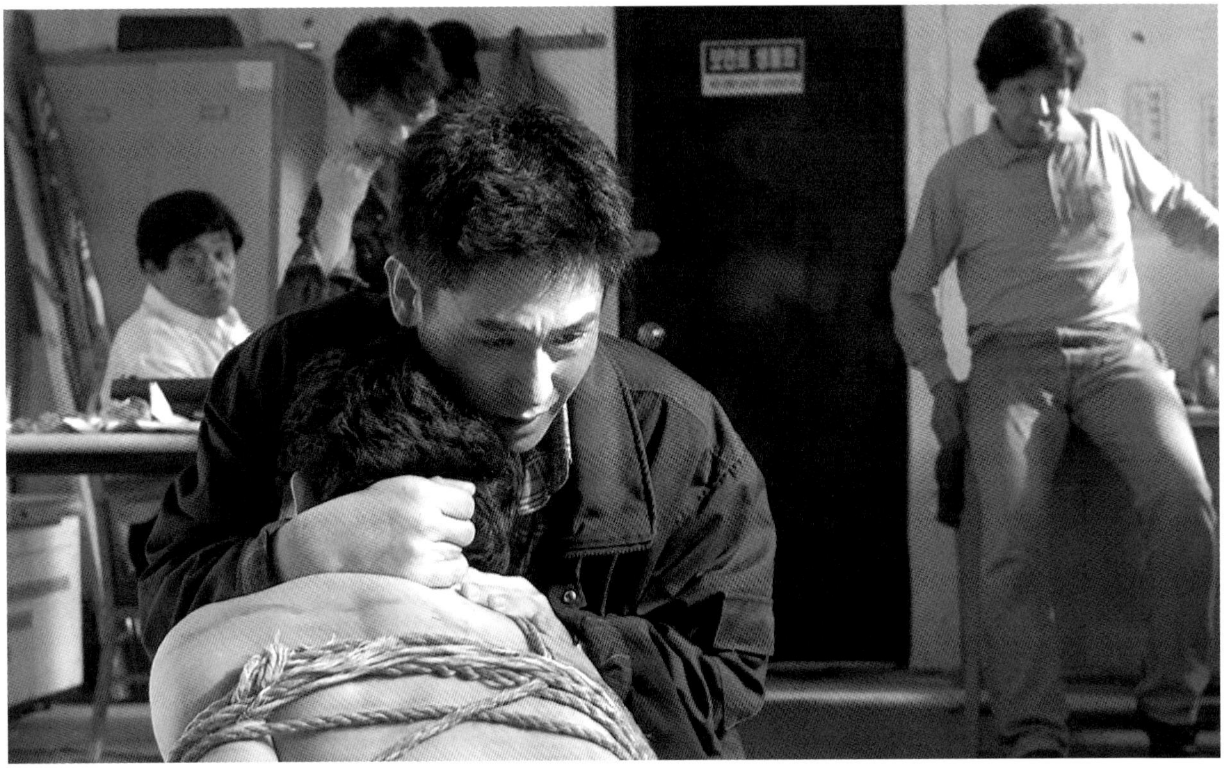

◀ 11

◀ 12

a living body; the disabled, paralyzed body becomes a dancing body, etc. Lee Chang-dong's films are populated by such bodies, which are never what they should be and never quite conform with social norms, but also above all are never identical to themselves: illogical bodies, deprived of identity or stability, bodies that are shaped and defeated by a shift towards invisibility, absence, unrepresentability, at the very moment when they are at their most present and visible. What is visible here is the effect on and in the body of the body's becoming, of its life and power; what is invisible is the body as unity and identity but also, and above all, the very process of becoming: we see the effects of this process on screen, but not the process itself. We do not see the openness, which remains out-of-frame, as it prevents the bodies from closing in on themselves and carries them away in a crazy dance, a deep, irrational, imperceptible transformation. When, in *Oasis*, the body of the disabled girl suddenly and momentarily transforms into a valid, dancing body, no explanation is given, no rationalization is proposed. The shift from one body to another is delivered via a wrong match, a camera movement that establishes this discontinuity and asserts it as such without any reference to an explanatory context. Other directors could shoot Lee Chang-dong's scripts, and one can well imagine what Ken Loach would do with *Poetry*'s script... Other filmmakers – another cinema – would fill the gaps, reduce the differences, remove the inconsistencies, either by summoning up believable causal relationships and explanatory systems, or by justifying the wrong match by a character's imagination, dream or delirious subjectivity. On the contrary, even when Lee Chang-dong appears to adopt this kind of rationalizing perspective, he still strives to leave the gap open, to highlight the discrepancy, to preserve irreconcilable fragments and to maintain wrong matches. This process involves an entire aesthetics as well as an ontology, ethics and politics – an economy of bodies whose strangeness, incoherence, abnormality and irrationality are valued and asserted: unruly bodies for a positively dark thought that calls for a different cinema as well as different bodies, ways of thinking and spectators: a different world...

The sleepwalking spectator

Burning is not only a film to watch, a show that stands at a distance from the spectator: the spectator's body, their perception and mind are part of the film. The viewer is no longer facing the film as if facing an external and alien spectacle: they are in the middle of the film, lost in a world that affects them and forces them to wander. This could

◀ 13

undoubtedly apply to Lee Chang-dong's cinema in general, but it does in a particularly acute and radical way to *Burning*. This film challenges vision and the visible at the highest level. It erodes the power of the gaze, of the eye: the power to produce distance and presence, to produce a spectacle, reducing what is seen to a panorama and a set of visible qualities, to create a subject of the gaze from which and for which the world is deployed as visible. It could be that what we are saying here is not entirely accurate: is it not the purpose of any film to try to reduce the gap between itself and the viewer, to draw them into the film (identification), to influence their thoughts, emotions and feelings? Usually, the quality of a film is measured by its ability to attract the viewer into the film. However, this inclusion of the viewer and the action of the film over their mind and body often relies on clichés, on the film's conformity to predefined physical or mental patterns, which leads not to disorder or loss, but to the consolidation of clichés and habits, to the reactivation of usual connections to the self and to the world. In Lee Chang-dong's work, it is the opposite: the aim is to act on the viewer and immerse them into the film, but in order to unravel clichés and patterns of the body and mind, to get them lost and paralyzed, to unravel their body and mind, to lead them to a point where they are caught up in the chaos of the film and become something else than what they were. The spectator finds themselves in the situation of the protagonist in *The Charterhouse of Parma*: first of all an observer, at a distance from a battle in which he is suddenly caught up and in which he only perceives chaos, disorder and incomprehensible signs, losing himself in the heart of this world that he no longer looks down to, that he no longer sees, that explodes into general incoherence. The optical relation is no longer panoptical: the visible is inhabited by the invisible and the unthinkable, it is fragmented into a totality without unity, into an incoherent sum of partial points of view that cannot add up or be reduced to a unified narrative with a central and centralizing subject. The world explodes and the spectator is blind. *Burning* highlights this experience – both cinematographic and existential –, inviting the viewer to adopt a different relation to the world and to themselves, where the world is no longer obvious. The «subject» of this experience no longer knows what they see, no longer knows how to think or what there is to think.

Lee Chang-dong's films recurrently feature characters who are caught up in this experience: sleepwalkers or automatons who find themselves caught up in a story they don't understand, don't perceive and can't really think, like Jongsu in *Burning*, who works as a stand-in for the spectator. A filmmaker like Spielberg is always at the limit of this experience but chooses to remain within a panoptic relation to the world, preserving the spectacular nature of the world and a subject for whom and from whom this show can exist. His films feature the emergence of an event that throws the world into chaos: aliens, dinosaurs, Nazis, etc. But the characters, by their actions, extract themselves from this chaos, suppress it and end up as heroic winners, always remaining, in one way or another, remote spectators. The world order has been disrupted but this order is restored and the spectator always emerges healthy and safe from the worst situations. Through the film and the actors, they can continue to be a valid and intellectually self-controlled hero. In Spielberg's films, we emerge alive and intact even from the Shoah: the world remains only a spectacle of which we are the remote heroes. And ultimately, Spielberg as a filmmaker remains like the character of Oskar Schindler who stands on a hilltop, perched on his horse, contemplating the spectacle of a Nazi raid from a distance while understanding its meaning, logic and ins and outs: what he sees does not overwhelm him but on the contrary reactivates his power to see and to understand.

On the contrary, Lee Chang-dong – along with his characters – follows Rossellini's path: that of neo-realism, which has been explored in a particularly thorough and brilliant way by Fellini. His characters are like Guido Anselmi in *Eight and a Half (8½),* or Snàporaz in *City of Women*, and ultimately like all the characters invented by Fellini: they are ghosts wandering through a fragmented and inconsistent world that they can neither think nor see from a panoramic point of view since this world is always different, enigmatic and challenging – a series of hallucinatory images that are nevertheless the reality of this world far beyond what can be rationalized, understood, imagined, perceived, appropriated or controlled. Fellini's cinema deploys and explores this world, like that of David Lynch and that of Lee Chang-dong. All three filmmakers create a spectator who is absorbed in a world where they can only wander and get lost, like a ghost and like a ghost's unprecedented, subversive body. In *Burning*, Ben's appearance alongside Haemi is not accompanied by an on-screen contextualization, and the story of their encounter in Africa, a story told by the two characters, cannot therefore be fully proven. Who is Ben? What is the exact nature of the relationship between him and the young woman? What is the purpose of their acquaintance with Jongsu? We do not know and cannot know it. And the impossibility of this knowledge is precisely what Lee Chang-dong is aiming at. The same applies to the nature of the relationship between Ben and Jongsu, and between him and Haemi. And if we do not know, is it not also because, in this instance, the body

14 ▶

has been evicted? The bodies of the actors, the characters they embody, are not staged in such a way as to show their encounter, and the eyes of the spectator do not see this encounter. Sight, the only means of certainty (a means that is reversed in *Burning*, since what we see is on the contrary presented as uncertain and irrational), is disqualified. The body is produced as absent, and the body's absence, in action or perception, generates the fundamental uncertainty of this narrative thread, as well as that of the whole film. There is no vision or panoptic gaze in Lee Chang-dong's work but partial images, images that are fragments of images. The spectator does not see everything, and the lack of vision imposed on them implies a form of blindness in their gaze, just like it implies in a form of ignorance and uncertainty in their thinking, something that can be grasped neither by the eye nor by the thought.

When watching the film, we do not understand what is happening, what we see or the thread of this ever-shifting story. In *Burning*, as probably in all his films, Lee Chang-dong creates an irrational cinema, or at least one that escapes the usual rational patterns. What does the incendiary drive mean? Is it a drive? Do any fires really happen? Or are they only a fantasy and a lie? Is Haemi for real? Is her sexual relationship with Jongsu purely fantasized? The questions multiply precisely because the filmmaker's point is to produce questions and to produce thought – both in the mind of the spectator and in the film itself, as a film is also thought in action. This thought is first and foremost made of questions: it is a thought without answers, for which the usual answers become ineffective, a thought essentially composed of questions for a world that is by definition enigmatic, separated from the knowledge through which we usually think and relate to it. A thought that is associated with belief, a world that cannot be known, that can only be an object of belief...

Social body and «abnormal» body

Despite what we have said, bodies in *Burning* seem to have a high visibility. It is not simply that the bodies are visible and present, that the two actors and the actress are actually on screen (except when the latter disappears...). It is also that the bodies we see, which are also social bodies, are characterized by a certain mode of existence: they are the signs of the social order that constitutes them, they bear the signs of this social order and integrate its norms, and can be defined through these norms. These bodies are expressions of what the social order does to bodies, namely to reduce them to a set of

15 ▶

visible signs. In *Burning*, the visibility of bodies is that of a social system that reduces the body to a set of visible and normalized characteristics. During a scene where she meets her childhood friend Jongsu, Haemi appears to conform to a role, a body language and a physical appearance that are entirely gendered and compliant with the norms attached the female gender. Her body is shaped by socioeconomic hierarchies. She works and must strive to do what the work is supposed to do, namely produce wealth for the owners of the work. She mimics excitement, performs choreographed and stereotypical gestures that are easily understandable –stereotypical, and therefore determined by others, as the expression on her face or her speech. In this context, Haemi appears as an immediately significant and understandable body, an issuer of social signs, subject to a social order that shapes and directs it.

Lee Chang-dong appears to want to deliver a critique of South Korean society, with its growing consumerism and subjection to the imperatives of neoliberalism. At the same time, he delivers a version of the body that appears determined by social, political, economic and cultural factors: the body is only a set of visible signs of this global social order, and its sole status is that assigned to it by this order. It is above all the exhibition of what the social does to the body: reducing it to its visibility, to a set of signs that inform the body and make it intelligible, manipulable and useable. The social order traps the body in visibility and in a system of meaning that is based on this visibility. It produces bodies that are adequate to this visibility - gestures, expressions, postures, clothes, sexuality, gender, etc. - and subjects the bodies to this regime of exclusive visibility. This body is the common body that we meet in public spaces, it is the body of common representations of the body, the truth of the body in the psyche, it is the body of commercial art and *mainstream* cinema, even when the *mainstream* can have the appearance of auteur or protest cinema. This body subjected to the neoliberal system of visibility corresponds to a certain system of signification in which the signs are immediately and entirely obvious, signifying, manipulable – signs that are the effect and the vector of a power. For this reason, many films are difficult to watch and to accept and cause weariness and disgust: they are the standardized products of power and are in themselves a power that aims to submit us.

In *Burning*, Lee Chang-dong stages this normalized and hyper-visible body, apparently reduced to its visibility. The three actors are beautiful in an obvious way. Their beauty corresponds to the current norms: youth, thin, athletic, etc. The characters carry with them and in them the signs of their social belonging, of their position in the economic and social hierarchy. Clothing is of course a social marker: more or less luxurious, more or less adapted to the context, social function, gender, etc. Ben's discreetly luxurious clothes contrast with Jongsu's jeans and T-shirts, with the clothes he wears when he wades in manure to care for his cow (Ben is on the contrary a city dweller). But as a social and defining marker of the body, clothing can also be the sign of a gap from what is expected within a particular social and cultural framework. In *Burning*, Ben's clothes express his belonging to the wealthy class, in contrast to Jongsu's; but in *Oasis*, the character of Hong Jongdu, an essentially ill-adjusted man, first walks around in a shirt in the middle of winter while all the others wear anoraks and coats: he appears to live in a different time and a different dimension from the others – which he does. His presence introduces a gap from common reality, another place and another way, which cannot blend into what exists and is possible here.

In *Poetry*, the grandmother's elegance is surprising because it does not match what is expected of a cleaning lady. In *Secret Sunshine*, Lee Sin-ae's understated clothing contrasts with her hair style which makes her look like a «madwoman» (which she is), in a seemingly hyper-normal and normative society, a society to which she has made the effort of belonging (and failed). Clothing extends and defines the body, its adaptation or maladjustment, its internal states and what affects it: it is treated as a sign of the body. It is a signifier of what happens to it, what it endures, what constitutes it, its identity or its disorder. Clothing signifies what the body has incorporated – social conditioning – to become what it is, its submission to this order as well as the power that is bound to it within it. However, it also signifies the discrepancy with this order, the state of an «abnormal» body, in rebellion or in flight, a body that exists elsewhere and introduces this elsewhere into a whole that does not want it.

An extreme case of this use of clothing is paradoxically the absence of clothing: nudity, as in the scene in *Oasis* where Jongsu and Han Gong-ju make love (a similar scene appears in *Poetry*, when the grandmother has sex with the elderly man who is also disabled). The fact that these two bodies are naked, that the characters are two individuals with physical and psychological disabilities, is literally unthinkable for those who catch them in the act: these bodies reveal an extraordinary desire that transgresses established codes, revealing a reality of the body that escapes social assumptions and prejudice. These bodies are, within this context, intolerable and incomprehensible. So much so that, in order for this event to be processed and for a reaction to be possible – and for the sensory-motor link to be restored – this intolerable and incomprehensible event is forced through the prism of the group's rationalizing codes and relations: the situation is interpreted as rape – which is in a sense, what the *visible* dimension of the image makes it appear like – and not as the visible manifestation of a desire that possesses these bodies and is their invisible secret.

This sociological and cinematographic logic of the body is also found in everything that is associated with the body, everything that is connected to it as a more or less immediate and obvious dimension: objects, jewels, cars, etc. The same goes with easy or clumsy movements, gestures and postures, with ways of living and moving in space, of owning it through the body. The body is indeed a social product and a social sign, as much as it is in itself the exercise of a social power, of what is subjected to this power, of what this power requires. The characters' ways of walking, sitting, standing and looking show so many different states of the body in relation to power – possible bodies within a power relation. Similarly, places act as kinds of prostheses of the body and as extensions of its social nature: they can be cramped or vast, opulent or « shabby » (to quote a character from *Oasis*), private or public, etc. In Lee Chang-dong's cinema, the body's relation to space is a relation to itself, to what it is or can be within a determined social framework, within a certain relation to power/power relation. The body's relation to space acts as a sign of this relation and of the possibilities that it creates for the body. Lee Chang-dong stages what we also learn from sociology: the body is a social construct, which exists within a set of asymmetric social relations that the body is required to incorporate to be what it is. It is the manifestation of these relations and of the power that constitutes them.

If the body is what acts or is likely to act, it is also what endures and is endured: it endures and is shaped by social order, it endures what this order predisposes it to endure. In Lee Chang-dong's films, insistent attention is paid to women's bodies. *Burning*'s female character is not the only one to be affected by exploitation, to endure a particular form of exploitation (even though this character also uses her body and its sexual power to reproduce a form of domination over the character of Jongsu). In Lee Chang-dong's work, this exploitation is the fate of many female characters. The female body is defined and perceived in different social, cultural and historical contexts as an object of sexual, domestic and economic exploitation. A young girl is raped by six boys and a grandmother ends up being sexually exploited – after being exploited domestically, socially and economically by her grandson, daughter and employer. A disabled girl is instrumentalized by her family to secure housing or money in compensation for her

16 ▶

17 ▶

◀ 18

◀ 19

◀ 20

alleged rape. Another rape, a real one this time, which leads to the suicide of a girl, is expected to be compensated by money. In another film, the male environment is in a position of sexual domination over women. In this systemic logic, the female body is seen as an object, something that is used by the male establishment but also by the economic and social establishment (in *Burning*, the female character is the object of a rivalry between the two men, and the stakes of this competition are just as erotic as they are social and economic). The body is reduced to the status of an object, in so far as it appears exchangeable and often finds itself part of a pure logic of commercial exchange. Like the body of the proletarian according to Marx, it serves as a source from which a quality is extracted for profit and, more generally, for pleasure: a liberal or neoliberal body, a dehumanized body, a body as abstract market value, a body dominated by the masculine and by money, etc.

It could be that Lee Chang-dong is delivering a critical diagnosis of contemporary South Korean society. His diagnosis could encompass the global logic of current neoliberalism, of which prostitution or violent appropriation are models. It is certainly relevant to gender relations in today's South Korea, but it also reaches far beyond. The fact is that Lee Chang-dong films the effects of these economic and sexist systems on and in women's bodies, on and in bodies in general. He films the ways in which these systems shape them, what they do to them, how they define them within power relations and how they grant them different qualities that allow them to exercise or endure power. If Lee Chang-dong endeavors to show the visible effects of this social and political logic of the body, it is in order to diagnose it, to deliver a critical point of view on this logic, to make it visible, thus disturbing its usual perception and understanding which imply, precisely, to not perceive it as a logic of domination. Lee Chang-dong's purpose is also to use this logic to explore filmic issues, the same issues with which he creates his own cinema.

The point is to show what is not seen, but also to film the visible effects of a system which in itself is not immediately visible, and to show the opacity of what commonly appears simple and obvious: cinema shows things and brings things into sight, all the while showing that what is usually seen cannot be reduced to this visibility. Lee Chang-dong is interested in establishing and bringing into sight causal relations that structure social relations. He is also interested in how power – both constitutive and endured – produces visibility and reduces things to their visibility. Women are perceived as such and are reduced to this perception, that is, to a set of visible qualities and signs that literally make them appear as exploitable objects. Similarly, Ben in *Burning* is reduced to the obvious signs of his wealth and to his normative heterosexual masculinity. In *Secret Sunshine*, the male and heterosexual order requires for men to exhibit (and only exhibit) the expected signs of dominant male heterosexuality. The grandmother in *Poetry* is essentially reduced by others to the signs that define her as woman, old, poor and a little eccentric – just like in *Oasis*, disabled characters are reduced by others to the visible characteristics and signs of their disability. The social order and power create the visible. They create the conditions for the visibility of the visible, and thus for exclusion from the visible, for restricting objects to a certain number of visible qualities that function as signifiers. Lee Chang-dong explores how social order and power create a framework of visibility, or a kind of visible surface that serves as a reality and as an object of thought: we see and think what is inscribed and can be inscribed on this surface, and the rest does not exist for us. In Lee Chang-dong's films, to varying degrees and in different ways, the body is the fundamental place of this inscription of the visible: socially, it becomes a readable, understandable and usable surface.

Invisibility and belief

Lee Chang-dong shows all this. However, if he remained at this level, if he remained within the limits of this socio-cinematographic point of view, then he would only comply with notions of the visible and of visibility that basically reproduce social order and its effects, even as he intends to denounce them. But Lee Chang-dong operates a series of subversive and liberating reversals, cinematographically (as well as socially and politically), as he strives to disrupt not only the visible but also visibility: the set of conditions that make the visible visible. The title *Secret Sunshine* is revealing in this respect: the sunshine, a phenomenon that is by definition hyper-visible and which is also the condition of visibility, is coupled with a secret, a darkness, an invisible unknown. The most visible thing and the condition for visibility contain in themselves an invisible, an elusive invisibility. The link between the visible and the invisible, between what makes seeing possible and its obscure double, is indeed an explicit theme of the film. What is seen is doubled by a dimension that escapes sight but is no less real, and forms part of a worrying, irrational and incomprehensible reality. In *Secret Sunshine*, what escapes the visible is initially associated with religion, with the codes and norms of the Christian system of thought and explanation: the invisible is God, the order of the world exists but eludes us, this order is defined by God's understanding which is inaccessible to us, the world must be an object of faith, everything belongs in a coherent whole. God is Totality,

물망초

22 ▶

the totalizing and unifying principle that allows the fragments we perceive to find meaning and coherence. And yet, in the film, this Christian explanatory discourse eventually appears for what it is: another way of rationalizing reality, of submitting it to a code, to pre-established and rigid norms. This discourse is a form of power and knowledge, not a belief that truly opens onto the invisible of the world. Even within this Christian explanatory system, the world is given as finite, obvious and precise. What is presented as visible is certainly not the totality of the world, but it can nevertheless be understood, thought, perceived as the visible signs of a cause that is invisible but remains namable, imaginable, and produces the world's coherence. The world is a Hollywood movie and God is Steven Spielberg. In *Secret Sunshine*, this false belief, this general and explanatory system collapses for the mother. For her, the world no longer has meaning, coherence or unity. What she sees of it no longer refers to an identifiable, socially defined and acceptable cause, to a processable and controllable code. There is no more Totality, no prospect of unity: the world shatters, imposes its fundamental darkness. Thought is dispersed, lost, and unable to bear what happens and corresponds to nothing. The mind is invaded by belief: not a form of belief that amounts to knowledge, but a true belief defined by uncertainty and non-knowledge, by the wandering of thought that thinks a chaotic world – or rather, that fails to think it. This belief is what is referred to as «madness» in *Secret Sunshine*, because it escapes the norms and conditions of thought, and because it differs from the way ordinary thought usually represents itself. This «mad» world takes over the character of the mother, dispossessing her of her thoughts and body, dragging her into the space of the invisible which forever disturbs the visible and the obvious. The film and the world become objects of belief, of blind contemplation that precludes knowledge – as in *Poetry* where the grandmother contemplates the flowers, the trees, the river and the fruit without having the words to describe them or a code to process them.

The image itself becomes double: what it makes visible has an invisible double. A film like *Oasis* could appear to contradict many of the ideas proposed here, since Hong Jongdu's body is omnipresent on the screen, often filmed in close-up, along with the signs that define this body and seem to reflect everything that this body is: the body of a mentally handicapped person, carrying the slight but visible stigmata of this handicap. The same is true, in a more pronounced way, for the body of the female character. Both are filmed from the front, in close-up, eminently visible, eminently present. The image seems simple, limited to what it shows, presenting itself as the means by which those who are not usually seen, or at least not looked at, who are usually excluded from the field of the visible (as in the restaurant scene), become hyper visible (image as a condition of the visibility of the visible). This dimension of image exists in the film in a powerful way, revealing what does not usually appear, and revealing the point of view by which what is not usually visible is nevertheless reduced to its visibility and to a set of signs that justify its exclusion. However, something else is also at stake because what is seen is always accompanied by a disturbance, a delay. This feeling is accentuated by the use of shaky camera, as if the characters were always about to run out of the frame or to unravel it, as if they could not be reduced to this frame: what we see of their body seems too narrow compared to what they are. The fact is that Hong Jongdu's character is unsuited to the norms, situations, socially constituted space, functions, moral and legal rules, and habits of relating to others. But this maladjustment remains a mystery, a secret buried in Hong Jongdu's mind and body. Why can't he understand the simplest, least complex job (delivery man)? Why does he always stray away from decisions and expectations, seeming to follow ideas and a logic that are never expressed? While Lee Chang-dong tries to film this body as closely as possible, he only films what is visible, always leaving off-camera (the off-camera within the field) the parts of the character that are perhaps not visible but could be articulated and explained. In this case, placing the focus on the visible is a way of subverting it by suggesting an invisible double (the mind, the body's internal states) that is fundamentally unthinkable and incomprehensible. And while the same applies to Han Gong-ju's body, the mystery that inhabits it seems even more disturbing: how can this body go through such contradictory and incomprehensible states, and undergo metamorphoses whose effects we see but which remain unexplained? What we see of this body is disconnected from its identity and from that of any other body. What we see of it involves an elusive invisible body, which exists off-camera but is nevertheless present in the image, although it is both invisible and inaudible. It is worth noting that Lee Chang-dong provides no element to explain this body and what happens to it through delirium or dream, or through a character's subjective point of view: the character's states are simply juxtaposed according to the logic of the wrong match, leaving the reason for what we see open and unknown. There is no unifying Totality, no meaning, no correspondence with what we know: there is only the visible and, at the heart of it, an invisible secret. And this secret is also that of desire, of love: the desire and love that connect these two beings. This desire is expressed in a sexual act that is perceived as rape when it conceals another truth, an unthinkable, invisible, unrepresentable truth, beyond everything else. The body «appears» in all its power because it can be affected: as well as being endured, it also endures what it conceals, the secret that inhabits it. The disability is of course endured, as are the inflamed shoulder or Alzheimer's disease that affect *Poetry*'s grandmother, as is the unbearable pain that seizes the mother in *Secret Sunshine*. But this passivity of the body is the sign of another deeper and essential passivity. The body is what happens to it, and what happens to it is also the most obscure, the least namable, listed, identifiable: an entire unconscious in the body - and the mind - that runs through it, shapes it, unravels it, tears it apart in incompatible directions, projects it out of the normal, of the codified, of regulated time and space. This is what happens to the body, the secret of a wandering body, inorganic but multiple, always outside and prey to an outside that shakes it and commands it. A body without God and without heroism, a body without a world, without meaning, without coherence, one that we cannot understand and in which we can only believe.

Oasis is the clearest illustration of what the body stands for in Lee Chang-dong's films and of the way in which he approaches the body intellectually and cinematographically: the body is the very place where the visible and the invisible are articulated, the paradoxical center from which the image is constructed in several dimensions. The first dimension concerns the visible, the presence on the screen of a visible body, which is *present* because it is visible. At this level, what is visible of the body is the result of social conditioning, a social process that produces the body's visibility. On a second level, this visibility is contradicted, disrupted, subverted by the emergence of an irreducible invisible. The body becomes not only an object of recognition but also of belief. Image, in Lee Chang-dong's work, is constituted by these two levels: image for presence, visibility, image of absence, invisibility. The most intense and beautiful moments are those in which the double image appears, the secret in the image, the inclusion of the invisible into the image. This image calls for a framing that includes what is out-of-frame – something out-of-frame within the frame. It also involves a type of editing that favors ellipses and wrong matches, as well as a certain type of non-linear, non-rational narrative and paradoxical temporality. All this creates the sense of a forever open, unrepresentable, unthinkable totality, whose outside is constantly repeated.

Believing in cinema

If *Burning* is a particularly powerful film, it is because it contains all the trends that make up Lee Chang-dong's cinema in the most concentrated and, in a sense, direct way. Lee Chang-dong does not tell one story but several – or rather, he arranges narrative threads that follow one another, blur and echo each other, each of which extends or

23 ▶

problematizes the others. The result is strange and undecidable. *Burning* is built on bifurcations: everything is different from itself, including the film itself, which never ceases to become something else than what it was. Everything exists by being absent, and persists through this absence.

At first, Jongsu runs into Haemi, a childhood friend whom he initially does not recognize. She is no longer the same: in addition to no longer being the child she once was, she has also had plastic surgery. Haemi is no longer who she used to be and appears as another version, another possibility of herself. While Jongsu considered her ugly as a child, when he finds her again, he is not indifferent to the pretty young woman she has become: a form of desire, a love story seems possible. Jongsu himself has changed physically and assumes a double identity: as a deliveryman and as a writer – or a wannabe writer: he is already a writer but not quite yet. The encounter that opens the film is marked by change and by the principle of the double: change with respect to oneself; being one's own double but a double that differs, that is not the same. The story that was theirs during childhood is transformed and takes another direction. This opening sequence concentrates the film's overall logic. While a relationship seems to be emerging between these two characters, its status is not clear: desire, revenge, manipulation, etc. The relationship can express either an attraction or a form of polite indifference, nascent desire and feeling or a casual hookup. When Jongsu and Haemi sleep together, their sexual intercourse is frenetic and cold, masturbatory and fusional. Jongsu is very turned on but at the same time distant, both an observer and a participant. Ambivalence prevails: this sex scene seems to juxtapose two different scenes, two different points of view on the same scene, two possibilities, two positions of Jongsu's character: spectator and actor, present and absent. The characters are double and the scene is double, distinct from itself, involving an absence, a world off-stage or out-of-camera, but which exists inside the scene or the frame, like a ghost that leaves a trace.

A third character, Ben, appears, whom Haemi is supposed to have met during an improbable trip to Africa. The duo becomes a trio. The relationship between Haemi and Jongsu seems to take a different turn while that between Ben and Haemi is not clearly defined: is it love, friendship or something in between? Haemi's character becomes more complex and vague. Ben's appearance and status are ambiguous. Jongsu's position is still that of both a participant and a spectator. A second narrative thread begins, which questions and obscures the first, as the characters' positions and identities blur. The same applies to the other narrative threads that are juxtaposed with the first two. Each time, the new narrative segment is less a continuation of the previous one than a move, a departure towards something else. The relationship between segments is to do with discontinuity and difference, with the nomadism of the narrative, the characters, identity, place and situation: from one segment to another, and within one given segment, identities are not quite the same, or can even be reversed, as in the final scene.

Each new segment does not simply follow the previous one: it reworks it, works its way through it, challenges it, questions it, reinvests it in a kind of loop that destroys it and shifts it, transforms it into a persistent ghost. The previous segment is never considered simply as the past: it becomes a ghost in the present, transformed into a trace in the present, going from actual to virtual. This virtuality does not abolish it but rather makes it exist within the present, not as an actual, visible thing, but as a thing that has been and continues to haunt the present. The past persists in a virtual present, and the relation between this virtuality and the present of the image, of the narrative, transforms the past into something else: into something that it was not but is now becoming. *Burning* is a film about time: a film that complicates time, introducing this complexity into the narrative, images, identities and editing. The film's linear time is coupled with a temporal discontinuity, an erratic time that disrupts and problematizes the former. And this double temporality is itself met by another temporality, which is an effect as much as a cause of the relationship between the first two: a temporality that defines a kind of dynamic loop between the present and the past, between the current and the virtual, and by which the current and the virtual not only coexist but constantly switch from one to the other. The whole film is constructed according to this temporality, where what remains out-of-frame – the virtual – is constantly looming at the edge. Or rather, the film develops a multiplicity of out-of-frame worlds, distributed over different time strata and articulated with each other, constantly introducing the invisible into the visible, the unsaid into discourse, the imperceptible into perception – just like the cat that may or may not exist, or rather that both does and does not exist, just like greenhouses that are both burned and not burned. Just like the film which is simultaneously what happens *and* what is imagined and written by Jongsu, or which is quite different - the film as pure thought, a thought thought by no-one, as irrational and incomprehensible as the world itself, an impersonal, intangible body affected by unthinkable, unlivable movements and passions...

The same is true of the identity of the places, characters and relationships between the three main characters who are at the same time this or that, this and that within different temporal dimensions and points of view. The relationship between Jongsu and

Haemi is a relationship between Jongsu, Haemi and Ben and/or at the same time a relationship between Jongsu and Ben. Heterosexual desire can be and is homosexual desire. The murder can be and is the effect of a destructive impulse, the elimination of a rival, the fantasized realization of homosexual desire, etc. The final scene and those immediately preceding it, as well as Lee Chang-dong's editing, precipitate and concentrate all the temporal dimensions that define the film as well as what they imply about identities and narrative: everything clashes at a high speed, the whole film is suddenly redistributed, and notions like bifurcation, virtuality, out-of-camera space and the ghostly nature of this radical film emerge as major themes.

Lee Chang-dong films time as plural, multiple and complicated, which cinematographically produces a particular type of images, characters, stories, relations between what is seen and heard and what is out-of-frame, etc. With *Burning*, Lee Chang-dong assembles these effects of time beautifully, building a film from signs of the present, restoring our perception and understanding of this moment – an astounded understanding, collapsing into vertigo. If the world is time, then how can we experience it and think it? How can we live and think of a time in which what is also is not, in which this is also that and something else? How to experience and think this plural and multiple temporality? How to experience and think the time that runs through and arranges all of *Burning*'s strata and temporal dimensions - the time of becoming, the eternal present of becoming, the great out-of-frame floating throughout the film, like a ghost, both present and absent everywhere? What is this beyond that haunts Lee-Chang dong's films, this outside beyond totality, which constantly opens and undoes and destroys the Whole? Is it time, the process of becoming that carries everything with it? Is it the film itself, with its crazed logic? Or is it both: the film as a thing in the process of becoming, a sensitive plate, a torn body, a blind eye, the most unconscious of thoughts?

24 ▶

THE AESTHETICS OF DISAPPEARANCE

DIFFRACTED TIME AND INVISIBILITY

The Principle of Indeterminacy

From *Green Fish*, *Peppermint Candy*, *Oasis*, *Secret Sunshine* and *Poetry* to *Burning*, each film by Lee Chang-dong is structured as an open-ended piece. The narrative line is jagged, truth is covered by equivocation and objective data clashes with subjective worlds... It is not just that a single piece is missing, making it impossible to assemble the puzzle: rather, it is the entire puzzle – life as a puzzle – that is dislocated and hidden. The crystal of life is cracked and pervaded by the unintelligible. In this context the quest for *The Figure in the Carpet*, as in Henry James' novel, is no longer possible. In this unresolved universe, the investigation for a hidden motive becomes obsolete. The turmoil and bifurcations are irremediable: this dissonant world will not achieve resolution.

We should refrain from interpreting Lee Chang-dong's work through the prism of European philosophy, which is alien to him. However, his films could be read from the perspective of post-Leibnizism as conceptualized by Deleuze in *The Fold: Leibniz and the Baroque*. As in Borges' or Whitehead's works, Leibniz's universe of converging series, governed by the principle of the best of all possible worlds, has been eclipsed by a universe of divergent series. In this unstable world «where paths lead off in different directions» (Borges), the consonances between events have vanished and tensions can no longer be resolved. In the absence of any resolution or dialectical synthesis, the death of harmony opens the way for the proliferation of a multitude of juxtaposed and unverifiable hypotheses. The principle of verifiability ceases to operate, leading to the bankruptcy of a world where cracks and gaps cannot be closed, and where composite hypotheses cannot be reconciled.

Lee Chang-dong's aesthetics is based on a principle of uncertainty that brings to mind the rules that govern the quantum world[1]. Many of the protagonists in his films experience a sense of indeterminacy that borders on disorientation. They stumble against the opacity of reality and wander the world, oblivious to one of its dimensions while trying to grab at another.

Let us enter Lee Chang-dong's universe with his latest film and masterpiece: 2018's *Burning*. The motif of the palimpsest presides over the film's narrative construction: inspired by Murakami's short story *Barn Burning* (from his collection) and by a novella by Faulkner novella also entitled *Barn Burning*, *Burning* is composed of ghostly strata – a palimpsest of sources where the difference between the original and the copy is eroded[2]. Mixing heterogeneous levels of text, superimposing semiological sediments (erased traces, outcropped footprints...), the film plunges its protagonists into an existence that

[1] Developed by Heisenberg and also known as the principle of indeterminacy, the uncertainty principle stipulates that it is impossible to know both the position and the amount of movement of a given particle. One of the two dimensions escapes whenever the other is captured, making it impossible to know both physical properties simultaneously. This structural impossibility is nothing to do with the inadequacy of our epistemological resources.

[2] See "Le cinéma, art du fantôme : Lee Chang-dong» by Jean-Philippe Cazier, Diacritik, 24 September 2018.

feels like a palimpsest, composed of successive layers that erase each other. The film's palimpsestic nature mirrors the protagonists' experiences, which are geochronies: a palimpsests of layers (from the Greek for «scraped again»), like onion skins scribbled by a tangle of old and recent lines and eroded by the practice of rewriting. As Jongsu investigates the mysterious disappearance of Haemi, a young woman, the reconstruction of facts remains unclear. As the materiality of the data fades away, the young man's mind loses itself in conjectures that nothing ever validates or invalidates. Based on the convergence of a few clues, Jongsu's imagination secretes a scenario that he ends up translating into radical action. The young man puts an end to this indeterminacy by acting out: he murders Ben. The amplification of radical doubt, exacerbated by vague signs and murky convictions, leads to an irreversible act, which, although it eases an internal tension, does not rattle this sense of objective uncertainty.

With this disruptive act, this world governed by the principle of uncertainty moves to a different level of reality. Ben's murder at the hands of Jongsu marks the end of quantic fuzziness: the transition from microscopic to macroscopic reality.

To put an end to the unbearable feeling he experiences when faced with a fuzzy, erratic reality, Jongsu resorts to crime to settle the undecidable. Did Ben really commit murder? Should his plan to burn down the greenhouses be understood metaphorically? Is the greenhouse near Jongsu's father's farm that Ben plans to set on fire none other than Haemi? Is Ben a serial killer? Neither Jongsu nor the spectator will ever know. In a hallucinatory paper chase, eroded by the intertwining of concrete clues and fantasies, Jongsu engages in a mental investigation without ever confronting Ben directly.

«There is no fact, only interpretations»: the climate of the film brings to mind this sentence by Nietzsche. The self is mediated by the projective activity of consciousness, by the for-itself (*pour-soi*). The narrative system follows oblique movements. But if there is such a thing as a clinamen – i.e. a deviation of atoms falling into the void – it is one that preserves encounters between series of words and series of things. Deflection itself is deflected, and does not produce any significant collision as a result of the impacts. The word «greenhouse» continues to fall in the void without ever colliding with its reality.

Jongsu finds a childhood friend he doesn't recognize and falls in love with her, although he found her unattractive as a child. Their mutual attraction culminates in a night of love. As Haemi travels to Africa, Jongsu feeds her cat without ever seeing it. Upon her return from Africa, Haemi asks Jongsu to pick her up at the airport, but she is accompanied by Ben – a Korean Gatsby – whom she has met at Nairobi airport. Jongsu,

◀ 25

26 ▶

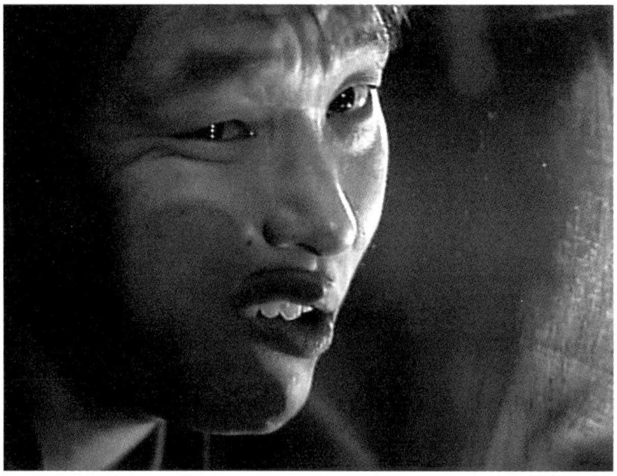

◀ 27

who is in love with Haemi, feels dispossessed from his love. The young woman is delighted by Ben's presence. Lee Chang-dong depicts the rivalries of a triangular relationship against a backdrop of antagonism between social classes. The humiliation of Jongsu, a delivery boy and apprentice writer, by a Porsche-driving golden boy feeds into a study of the violence that governs relations of social domination.

In *Burning* as in other Lee Chang-dong films (in particular *Secret Sunshine* and *Poetry*), the invisible is associated with three radically distinct registers. First of all, invisibility as a deficiency of perception: it can be connected to visual impairment or to narrow-mindedness and mental blindness; secondly, invisibility as transcendence, alluding to an unattainable higher mystery and to what exists beyond the field of perception; thirdly, invisibility as ecstasy, pursued as the object of a quest, a Mystical Grail coveted by the characters.

Jongsu's mental activity is entirely focused on the task of converting one form of invisibility into another. In a play between these three registers, Jongsu interprets the invisible as a sign for something else. There is for instance the mystery of the cat that hides in Haemi's apartment, and which Jongsu never sees. Jongsu then sees a cat run out of Ben's apartment and notices that the cat responds to the name "Choffo": he thus clings to the near certainty that Ben lied when he said that he had taken in a stray cat, and that this cat was actually Haemi's cat, Choffo. Ben's lie opens up a Pandora's box of guilt: a lesser evil (Ben lied) becomes the sign of a swarm of evils (Ben is a serial killer).

As Choffo can never be seen in Haemi's apartment, Jongsu and the spectator come to doubt its very existence. The cat is not alone in hiding and in remaining invisible, casting doubt on its reality. There is also the well that Haemi claims to have fallen into when she was a child, an event that Jongsu no longer remembers although Haemi claims that he had saved her life by pulling her out of the well.

The viewer's gaze is as disoriented as Jongsu's. A blind spot devours the field of vision. The retina is no more reliable than the intellect. Perception slips under the spell of imagination. Jongsu strives to draw lessons from what is hidden, assuming that an element of truth is contained in the invisible – for example, through the invisible bodies of the women that Ben allegedly killed. Did Ben throw them into the water basin whose surface he contemplates?

Haemi expresses what I call invisibility as ecstasy, a state the character aims for as the result of an initiation. From her journey to Africa and her crossing of the Kalahari desert, Haemi brings back a tribe's ritual: an ancient dance around a fire during which the initiate transitions from "Little Hunger" stage to "Great Hunger". A «Great Hunger» initiate has gained access to the invisible and communicates with the invisible powers, while a «Little Hunger» individual has not yet acquired this mystical knowledge. Haemi, who has travelled to escape and is expecting for communication with the spirits to give meaning to her life, performs the African tribe's « Great Hunger dance» for Ben and his friends.

Seeking evidence amid ambiguous clues in an attempt to see through their ambivalence and find their unequivocal content, Jongsu holds on to his realistic methods in a world that has ceased to be real. He is the prisoner of a vision of the world where things are connected by meaning and purpose, where logic draws its structure from the law of cause and effect. He seeks to separate true from false, which implies that in his eyes the dualism of true vs. false remains operative. Just like the viewer, Jongsu hunts down in vain the truth behind Haemi's disappearance. Ben tells him about his favorite hobby: burning a plastic-covered greenhouse every two months because he thinks these constructions deface the countryside. The barns in Murakami's short story have become these cylindrical plastic-covered greenhouses that deface the Korean countryside. Ben announces that the next greenhouse he will set on fire is not far from Jongsu's father's farm, so Jongsu travels across the countryside to see a greenhouse on fire but never finds one.

Jongsu cannot accept that reality is sinking into indecipherability. For him, the world must be readable or risk descending into chaos. However, in a world made of divergent series, no Champollion is around to interpret the hieroglyphs (whether those are visual or oral, like the threats uttered by Ben): the possibility of decryption is structurally blocked and invalidated from the outset.

No clear lessons can be drawn from the accumulation of observations, sensations and experiences. Posing as an anti-Bildungsfilm, *Burning* nevertheless draws one certainty from the inferno of doubt and confusion: confusion does not go away. There can be no narrative of formation, of learning signs as in *In Search of Lost Time*. No final revelation, no confession, no admission of guilt... The enigma persists in all its depth.

When Haemi vanishes without a trace, Jongsu soon suspects his rival and follows him. Ben finds him out and invites him into his flat. Jongsu then comes upon two clues – two "Rosebuds" – from which he draws the quasi-certainty of Ben's guilt: a pink watch in a drawer, which he thinks he recognizes as Haemi's, and the cat that runs out.

The sum of unspoken and unseen facts creates a growing sense of suspicion that builds up into an obsession. As Jongsu suspects Ben of having murdered Haemi, he stabs him and puts his corpse into his Porsche, which he then sets on fire. Both a physical and mental element, the motif of the fire is apparent throughout the story, from the blaze of Jongsu's mother's clothes to the burning car and the greenhouse fire that is expected to happen but never to be seen.

The murder closes the trajectory but does not appease the doubt, as the mystery remains whole: is Ben guilty? Where has the woman gone? Why doesn't she give any more signs of life? How can Ben's attitude be explained? Does the ambivalence of Jongsu's feelings towards Ben suggest fratricidal rivalry, repressed homosexual desire or class revenge? The questions remain open and unresolved. Ben's ambiguity is not dispelled.

If the film is constructed like a palimpsest of texts, it also exploits a sound scroll, a set of musical quotations, in particular with the appearance of music by Miles Davis for the score of *Elevator to the Gallows* by Louis Malle.

Diffracted and Divergent Temporalities

In Lee Chang-dong's films, the plots are subject to shifts from one story to another, as the narrative plays between nested, divergent and heterogeneous durations. The ghostly erosion of facts and their ontological incompleteness create a labyrinthine perception of time, marked by discordant directions. The time of aimlessness communicates with the aimlessness of time, when time goes out of control. The protagonists (grandmother Mija in *Poetry*, Yongho in *Peppermint Candy*...) stumble in the thickness of a multi-fiber temporality, in "stereoscopic" relief. Existential disorientation, which is reflected through temporal disorientation, provokes experiences of de-synchronization. Time is experienced as crumbled and diffracted because of the discrepancy between inner, subjective time and objective, external time, but also because of the absence of a match between diverse inter-subjective perceptions of time.

Each character is locked up in their own space-time reference frame, and experiences the other's reference frame as absolutely alien. Far from being connected by the fact that they belong to the same world, Mija's frame of reference is foreign to her grandson's and to those of the parents of the students who committed rape (*Poetry*); the series formed by Shin-ae does not connect with those of the inhabitants of Miryang (*Sunset Sunshine*). This double discrepancy (between the inside and the outside, and between different subjectivities) is often exacerbated by a discrepancy in the arrangement of the self (Yongho in *Peppermint Candy*, Jongsu in *Burning*). The characters' inner sense of time is also jeopardized under the assault of blurred perceptions. *Burning* pushes the superposition of non-congruent narratives and the clashes between reference frames to their very limit: its three characters each experience irreconcilable temporal segments.

Time is experienced as a tangled ball of wool, punctuated by asymmetries and bifurcations, and perceived as fundamentally alien because it is charged with ghosts and full of virtual layers where the past persists in the present.

In *Poetry*, in Mija's case, the fragmentation of time (in the sense of a fragmentation bomb) is accentuated by memory loss, diagnosed as a sign of early Alzheimer's disease. This is another instance of the figure of the palimpsest: no longer in its primary sense of an erased, reused parchment, but in its second sense of a psychological mechanism characterized by memory gaps and oblivion.Lee Chang-dong focuses on the outsiders, the marginalized, those who are left behind (Jongdu, a mentally handicapped delinquent and his lover, a young disabled woman in *Oasis*; the poverty of Mak-dong and his family in *Green Fish*...). He explores the rich psychological temporalities of the marginalized who live outside society, conversely denouncing the impoverishment, the alienation of linear temporality that occur when the world is governed by utilitarianism and profit, obsessed with work and performance. The fixed and objective time indicated by clocks has been forged as an instrument of human domination. In order to successfully alienate and domesticate beings and to standardize consciences, time had to be enclosed into the alienating form of Chronos. Against the violence of this perception of time associated with empty and deadly productivity are opposed poetry, creation and love, but also the relation to time that characterizes the voiceless and the excluded.

The orderly control of time was designed as a decisive tool for the training and enslavement of men. A translation of an impoverished, pathological and anemic relation to time, clocks stifle the experience of time. Linear time, vectorized by utilitarianism, is an agent of normalization that generates a biochrony to serve the interests of biopower.

Lee-Chang dong's films explore the crisis points that affect time in its countable, extensive, digital form. Far from the circular regularity of meteorological time and from the eternal return of seasonal time, Chronos is artificial and constructed time, free from the circularity of natural rhythm and seasonal cycles. The clock rules our bodies, devouring our existence. The acculturation and domestication of men requires that they subordinate themselves to the division of capitalized time. There can be no biocracy without temporal alienation, correlated to spatial alienation (prohibition of free nomadism, imposed sedentarity coupled with the promotion of regulated and profitable

28 ▶

forms of nomadism such as tourism...). The imposition of time management is the cornerstone of the generalized surveillance system that prevails in our societies of control: without this submission of the individual to the distribution of time, without this formatting imposed from childhood, there can be no training, no acculturation. Time must be internalized in its externalized and extensive form. Unable to distribute us freely in its folds, Chronos distributes us on a scale divided into past, present and future. Imposed objective time deprives us of subjective, perception-centered time. It robs us from the experience of time, separates us from our potentialities and from the construction of subjective forms. This time model is not only disenchanted, dehumanized and dehumanizing, but it is also decosmologized and decosmologizing: Chronos' objective time perpetuates the society of the spectacle.

Just like marginal love in *Oasis*, the perception of time associated with karaoke (in the sessions that punctuate Lee Chang-dong's films), reverie (in *Poetry,* Mija's attitude when encountering flowers or poetry), or writing in *Burning* escape the linear, productivistic and profitable vision of time. When connected to productivity, time becomes a symptom of nihilism: it hates chance, the notion of *"amor fati"*, and the perception of time as a « child playing dice» – in short, it hates life.

Lee Chang-dong's tenderness for those ignominiously called losers by the system makes them the only winners, as in a spiritual «loser wins». The outcasts of social success conquer islands of freedom through an experience of time that sidesteps both the Bible of performance and the ordeal of neoliberalism. Mija and the couple of lovers in *Oasis* embody the same purity as Parsifal or Dostoevsky's Idiot. Loaded with a political dimension, Lee Chang-dong's films take a critical look at class differences, inequality and injustice. He reactivates Spinoza's dualism between power and potency, where the world of potency shaped by the excluded is opposed to the world of power governed by the dominant.

The Aesthetics of Disappearance: Withdrawing Into Invisibility

Lee Chang-dong's aesthetics examine the beat, or more precisely the pulsation, that binds appearance with disappearance. His poetics question the resurge of appearance under disappearance, exploring the sense that it is «too late». In a floating world – the floating world of Buddhism and Japanese woodblock prints[3], where the stability of landmarks, things and recognition comes undone, the expectations of perception fall into pieces as absence corrupts presence.

[3] Ukiyo-e, 3images of the floating world») as investigated by Kazuo Ishiguro in *An Artist of the Floating World* - Faber and Faber (1986).

◀ 30

The sense that it is too late pervades many of Lee Chang-dong's films. In *Burning,* the world no longer makes sense in Jongsu's eyes: decomposed series can no longer be recomposed into a tangible, irrefutable truth. The truth is nowhere to be found. The young man's ability to understand and perceive is defeated. Jongsu, just like the spectator, understands too late – or never understands – that there is nothing to understand and that new relations to life and to its immanence can be invented: those should no longer be about sense or meaning, but about creating an art of encounters and consequences. No longer about hermeneutics, but about the experience of the power of living and thinking. The question: «What does this mean?» is replaced by: «What effects, what encounters, what tangle of individuals can this produce? » This pragmatic approach, focused on vital effects, fosters a new relation to the outside world.

In *Secret Sunshine*, Shin-ae understands too late the futility and uselessness of her gesture: going to prison to find her son's killer and grant him forgiveness. The murderer tells her that, as he has converted to Christianity, he has already received God's forgiveness. The murderer has been cleansed of his sin as God took away his guilt. Shin-ae understands too late the duplicity of the Christian church that had welcomed her, and sees how faith can be summed up as washing one's hands: a convenient alibi to avoid any moral issues. God, the higher authority, absolves sins and crimes. In *Poetry*, a rape is hushed by money while in *Secret Sunshine*, responsibility and conscience are stifled by faith and by the prospect of redemption.

The «too late» feeling is also the result of the discrepancy of temporalities and subjectivations. The ordeal of Shin-ae, an already widowed woman whose son is murdered, can be read as the parable of a Pieta-like figure. Devastated by the death of her son who has been kidnapped and murdered, Shin-ae takes refuge in the evangelical Christian religion and clings to her faith. The protagonist's existential trials reflect a mismatch of temporalities. While Shin-ae's thinking remains strictly tautological (this ray of sunshine is only a ray of sunshine, as in Gertrude Stein's formula «a rose is a rose is a rose is a rose»), the pharmacist in the small town of Miryang (whose name means "secret sunshine" in Korean) sees God's presence in this ray. For the proselytizing pharmacist, the ray of light gives us access to the transcendent, to the invisible world. After the murder of her son, Shin-ae, defeated and lost, abandons tautological thinking and converts to Christianity, seeking refuge in religion with its consolations and promises of an afterlife. She abandons her literal reading of life and discovers the four levels of reading of the Holy Scriptures defined by Christian translation: literal, historical, allegorical, tropological and anagogical.

In *Poetry*, Mija discovers too late that Wook, her grandson who spends his time watching television or surfing the net, raped a young girl with his schoolmates and that the girl then committed suicide. In her diary, the girl confided that she had been raped for months by six of her schoolmates, including Wook. The only response to Mija's scream of "Why did you do it?» is the disintegration of the «why?» – not because the characters have reached ataraxia as defined by Angelus Silesius («the rose is without why»), but because the lines of existence and thinking have been fatally disrupted.

An Ophelia-like corpse floating on the surface of the water, the girl has jumped off a bridge. The corpse drifts along the river. This inaugural drowning scene is a prelude to further drownings: Mija drowns in her failing memory, while her grandson drowns in the «banality of evil».

The poetry teacher teaches that «writing a poem is about seeking the beauty of what is in front of you». «You must write a poem. It is by writing that you will understand". But Mija's philosophy eventually concludes that an apple is not made to be looked at (or written into a poem), but to be eaten.

The «too late» feeling is due to the lack of communication between the closed universes of Mija and her grandson. Lee Chang-dong's work shows windowless monads that do not touch each other. Driven by her sense of justice, the monad Mija is alien to the fathers of the young criminals, who have chosen, in agreement with the school's head, to financially compensate the dead girl's mother in order to dissuade her from filing a complaint. No one listens to Mija's voice. When confronted with the power of money, the symbolic power of words is minimal: in this mercantile society, those without material wealth are considered as waste; they are nothing.

From Indeterminacy to Unresolved Suspense. The Confusion of Small Perceptions

The principle of indeterminacy forms part of the logic of irresolution, which is also the logic of unsolvability. The blurring of identity landmarks and levels creates an unshakeable state of disorientation. Complexity forms a labyrinth from which no-one can escape – be it from above, like Daedalus and Icarus, or from below via Ariadne's thread.

From spending time with Ben, Jongsu becomes consumed with hatred and suspicion. Because the narrative segments do not click together into a coherent whole, because the web frays into a kaleidoscopic movement, Jongsu tries to dispel the darkness of facts by committing murder. How can he bear his load and make his way in this vertigo

31 ▶

◀ 32

of signs? How can he react and find his place when the unrepresentable clouds what can be represented? How can he live in a realm of ghosts and disparities?

Intrigued by a young woman called Mi-ae, Mak-dong goes searching for her (*Green Fish*); Jongsu struggles with the enigma of Ben and Haemi (*Burning*); Shin-ae is dazed by the brutality of fate (*Secret Sunshine*)... In the grip of a swarm of confusing perceptions, these various characters struggle to achieve clarity, and attempt to focus their perceptive acuity on a detail or a dimension at the expense of others. In *Green Fish* and *Burning*, the strange focus of attraction, the object of the quest, is a young woman: the enigmatic Haemi, but also Mi-ae, a mysterious young woman in a red scarf that Mak-dong meets in a train and starts chasing. A nightclub singer, Mi-ae turns out to be the lover of the leader of the Bae Tae-kon gang. Mak-dong then becomes a member of the gang and climbs the social ladder in the world of crime.

Wook, Yongho and the murderer in *Secret Sunshine* have in common the narrowness of their soul, and the minimal scope of their consciousness. In Lee Chang-dong's universe, the sacrifice of the damned eventually appears as gratuitous and useless, because it does not improve the overall balance or harmony. The importance of the motif of light in *Burning* (atmospheric light, interior light, blazing flames, blue light) is present both externally when the film records the bifurcation of light from autumn to winter, and internally with Jongsu revolving around a black hole that stands for Haemi's disappearance.

A virtuoso mime and an expert of imagination, Haemi mimics the peeling and eating of a tangerine. Are the film and reality like the tangerine that Haemi pretends to peel and eat? When we peel off the visible, do we find the mystery of the invisible, the mystical heart of things? Or, on the contrary, is it by peeling off the invisible and working our way through the layers that we can access the visible?

The ambiguity that shrouds situations and beings causes misunderstandings. People wrongly believe that Shin-ae is rich because she wants to buy land in the village of Miryang. The inhabitants of Miryang have a distorted perception of the widow: based on scattered clues and false assumptions of Shin-ae's wealth, the professor schemes to kidnap her son. Another example of the ambiguity of the visible: the beauty of the young man's hands in *Peppermint Candy* conceals the murders they committed.

Jongsu does not know what happened to Haemi, and is unable to go through the grief process. Reality dissolves in a montage of foggy and imprecise signs. Lost among meaningless clues, the characters sway in a precariously built reality.

◀ 33

Things remain suspended, mental images collapse, the past percolates through the present and the possibility of a center crumbles… The unthinkable resides at the heart of the thinkable and the invisible rises to the surface of the visible. Discrepancies make it impossible to integrate perceptions into a clear macro-perception. An inner link connects perceptual confusion, plural temporalities and the wanderings of memory.

Did Jongsu forget that he once saved Haemi from the well into which she had fallen as a child? Or did Haemi dream up this fact? Bathed in fog, memories become ghostly and impalpable: there is a correlation between the failure of remembrance and the impossibility of piecing together a coherent and logical narrative. The failure of the character's initial recognition (Jongsu does not recognize Haemi, a former classmate, who has had cosmetic surgery) highlights the failure of reminiscence or subsequent investigation. Similarly, Shin-ae's trajectory seems predestined by an initial event: the breakdown of her car when she arrives in her deceased husband's home village. It seems as if the breakdown is an adverse sign that inaugurates all the failures and misfortunes to come. In response to their feelings of disorientation and loss, some protagonists surrender and act out, whether suddenly or after a long preparation, as if by giving death they could revive life and temporarily interrupt the general blurring of signs – in what is perhaps one last desperate attempt at making the world less nebulous and restoring its clarity for a short while.

Peppermint Candy questions the aftermath of the military dictatorship in South Korea by retracing the story of a man who has just committed suicide after having committed torture. The film looks back over twenty years of his life as a member of the repressive forces, seeking clues in the past to shed light on Yongho's suicide. Through the trajectory of Yongho, a young man who becomes an executioner, a criminal soldier and then a police officer, through Wook who commits collective rape, or through the cruelty of the murderer of Shin-ae's son, Lee Chang-dong stages explosions of violence that do not serve any individual or collective cathartic function. Death is gratuitous and does not help resolve tensions. Murder does not restore balance or bring peace – unlike catharsis, which, through the purging of passions, pacifies a situation of crisis.

A beacon of resistance to the contemporary world's collapse into the virtual, Lee-Chang-dong's cinema counters the disintegration of reality under the rise of generalized simulacrum by staging a quest for the invisible, which operates as a double for the visible. The invisible shines off camera like a «secret noise», providing a reference point for reality, a stopping point that can locally contain the empire of the virtual. The invisible appears as a space that eludes the tyranny of the visible: a breathing space, a void that escapes the saturation of images and the dogma of fullness.

◀ 34

◀ 35

36 ▶

◀ 37

38 ▶

ART AND THE PEOPLE

*I*n 2000, when I got off the plane to Jeonju, in south-central Korea, where I was supposed to help organize the newly created film festival, an old Korean friend told me: you have to see Lee Chang-dong's films. That same evening, on his television, he showed me the VHSes of *Green Fish* and *Peppermint Candy* that had just been published. My friend was very excited, as were many Koreans I knew, whether they worked in the film industry or in underwear manufacturing. Although I had been seeing Korean cinema for almost ten years, this was the first time I had noticed such a craze for films that seemed unattractive, even austere compared to those of Kim Kiduk or Hong Sang-soo, two directors who were already known internationally. A year later, I met Lee Chang-dong in the flesh, when I went to take up my position as a visiting professor at the Korean National University of Arts in Seoul. It was 2001, and my future office was still under construction, so I shared the office with Lee Chang-dong who had just successfully directed *Peppermint Candy* and had become a lecturer in the film department at the same university. Always friendly and distinguished, he placed his books on the right of his desk while mine were on the left. But there was nothing symbolic about that. We had a mutual friend, director Park Kwang-su, who was also part of the same faculty and had long been at the forefront of the new wave of Korean cinema in the late 1980s and early 1990s. We then met every year, most often during the Busan festival or in unusual circumstances such as a meal in Lyon with Cannes festival officials – as I officiated as a delegate for the International Cannes Critics' Week –as well as Korean officials and a couple of film critics. Then, after Lee Chang-dong had briefly held the post of Minister of Culture of his country, I met him again when a documentary was shot about his tour of France and Korea following the translation of one of his books. When *Secret Sunshine*, in my opinion his most accomplished film, was released, I came up with the idea of making a book about his films. After a wild conversation in an elevator after a screening, he accepted.

Time has passed, and now another opportunity arises for this book, at a time when Lee Chang-dong is at the top of his international fame and shortlisted for an Academy Award for *Burning*. Meanwhile, I had moved to Seoul and met his producer brother, in Hongdae's fashionable neighborhood in the central-eastern part of the megalopolis, where we both had liked to spend some time. As Lee Chang-dong was overloaded with interviews and trips for the promotion of *Burning*, I wondered if he would agree to embark on this book project. I was all the more worried because I had heard him say: «I don't like to explain the meaning of my films (...). Yet, I need to take care of promotion (...). The problem is that I like explaining things because I used to be a teacher. So I'm

39 ▶▶

good at this kind of exercise». Eventually (and fortunately) he accepted the project, «because of Antoine» he told me during our first interview. I then bowed my head, in the Korean way, to show my esteem. The brothers' offices, located ten minutes from my home, made things easier. Despite a planning error, because of a Korean holiday that none of us had noticed, we started the operations.

I have a difficult relation with interviews with directors. As a historian, I consider intentionality, what the filmmaker says about his works, as one of many discourses; a discourse to which little credit should be given; a discourse that can even divert attention from what really is in the film. And this, not to mention the promotional arsenal, the approaches strategically negotiated by distributors and which filmmakers are almost bound under contract to respect, etc. As a historian, I know that it takes time to access liberated speech. In this regard, I often quote Brian de Palma and his biographical documentary where, at over 74 years, he lets out things that had never been said about his own films. Finally, I would like to add a touch of local color: the art of politeness practiced by the Koreans who know how to adapt to the questions of foreign journalists so that everyone can leave the interview in good terms.

To return to the preparation, I knew that Lee Chang-dong had answered a good hundred interviews in the previous months. I had seen him and heard him complain about the repetition of the same questions from journalists, who were just going through the usual motions. The international press was buzzing with phrases like «filming the invisible», «hearing the inaudible», and the expected sophisms and circumventions, many of them crypto-metaphysical, which failed to describe how sexy that little Asian girl is in *Burning* when she dances naked in the sunset, bathed in cannabis vapors (which points to the regular success, in our countries, of Asian films with young naked women). There were many pitfalls, so I had prepared topics that could be discussed obliquely as well as a number of indirect questions. For example: "Nam June Paik said that it was no longer necessary to add more images in a world that is full of images that makes no sense. What is needed is to reorganize the existing images to give them meaning. Do you agree with this statement?" Or more historically: "During the Dresden uprising in 1846, Bakunin proposed to take all the paintings out of the museums and place them on the barricades with him and the revolutionaries. He expected that would make the king's soldiers think twice before they shot them. Is art in its rightful place today?" Or more avant-garde: "Your films seem to want to stimulate the viewer's awareness of their own daily life. Guy

Debord wrote that cinema replaces not only reality, but also political action. It consumes the desire for action while creating it. The viewer can see injustice on screen, think about it, and then go home peacefully, as if these kinds of films were enough to stop them from feeling guilty about the (bad) way the world is going. What do you expect from the viewers of your films?" Scriptwriter Kim Sung-tae who accompanied me had read my questions, and he was convinced that Lee Chang-dong would gape in surprise when he read them. My questions had to be reworked into something more similar to traditional Korean interviews. It was, in fact, too much to ask to engage in such discussions (even if Lee did, in part, answer these questions in another way). In spite of myself, I had fallen into the pitfall of trying to build up a discourse on the intentions of films that were self-sufficient. By the way, I remembered that I sometimes quoted Lee to my Korean students in their filmmaking class. They had boundless respect for his aura as Minister of Culture and for his academic way of communicating. I usually stress out my students when they present their short film project. To those who give me a long and verbose explanation of the film, I say to them: "All right, you don't need to shoot this film anymore: I understand everything!". I then add that the respected Lee Chang-dong himself said: "If I could explain my films with words, why would I make films?". This character's speech contrasts with that of the majority of local professionals, and he enjoys both the right to public speech and to be listened to in South Korea. Lee himself said: "People recognize me but (...) my films are only seen by a few people. I'm famous on paper. But I want to hear that my films are popular."

Over the years, shamelessly taking the opposite stance from film lovers and official critics who are quick to praise the mystique of genius, Lee has emerged as a filmmaker who could be described as pragmatic, almost down-to-earth in his approach to film production. This appears when he said with disarming sincerity, after the release of *Peppermint Candy*: "I lost 300 million won (about 200,000 euros) on *Green Fish*. With Peppermint Candy, I'll lose up to 500 million (about 400,000 euros). If I keep losing money, no one will want to invest in my next projects anymore." Or: "If you want to make a film, you need money. And for that, you have to convince and cheat. Afterwards, you just nervously wait for the results of the box office. You try to be strong, serene, but it doesn't work. I'm not in favor of films that only reach a small number of people. I want to make films that touch the general public." About his financing strategies, Lee says that "financing is based on the scenario. So I write the best that I can, pretending that I'll be able to shoot all of it."

40 ▶

◄ 41

◄ 42

Lee's awareness of the film industry, of the conditions of production that are inseparable from artistic creation, sometimes seem to produce a disillusioned vision of cinema. He once declared, for example, that: «when you prepare a film, everyone (the team) thinks they are an author, an artist. But when the shooting starts, it all turns into very physical slave work". This explains why, after each film, Lee expresses his desire to retire from cinema: "Sometimes, there are situations in a shoot where it is necessary to hurt each other, to stop collaborating in order to obtain a good result. I find this very disturbing. I'm seriously thinking about stopping making films." His refusal to delude himself extends beyond the mere making of the film: it reveals, behind his modesty as a communicator, his frustrations as a perfectionist idealist. For example, when he says: "I don't think you can communicate through a film (...). A film is neither conceptual nor physical. It is only an illusion. (...) When people read literature or a play, they believe that the meaning exists beyond the text. That is why there is an open space for communication. A film lover does not believe that there is anything beyond the film itself." This pessimism appears again when he explains (after saying: "I was disappointed at the low audience for my novels"): "After my dissatisfaction as a writer, there is one thing I know: I don't believe in Korean readers, I don't believe in the public, I don't believe in voters." Then he adds: "I have always felt desperate about life. What should we share with each other?" Nevertheless, Lee finds hope when he evokes, in dotted lines, his search for perfection and beauty: "(In a film), the invisible 1% decides everything. It is this 1% that makes the 99% finally add up to 100%. It's not easy, but you have to see this 1%." And about shots: «There is a line between a good shot and a poor shot. It's hard to explain what the difference is. Especially during a shoot. The team has to read my face, non-verbal communication." And he adds, about the atmosphere and relationships that make creation possible on a film: "If you have to explain everything to everyone, then you're screwed." One can imagine the tension of his collaborators when he had to explain to them that "in *Poetry*, the observation of the surrounding space is a search for beauty. A beauty experienced personally, not a common beauty. That's why the actress' perspective is important in this film."

Right from the start of his filmmaking career, Lee has been perceived as a writer. And yet, his vision is purely that of a filmmaker when he evokes filmic language. "I think that film is the best medium to show something of the human being. People can be separated from their social, political and economic context. They fight against their own reality. This struggle is what brings meaning to their lives." Lee Chang-dong snaps back at those who see his work as a way of bringing literature and cinema closer together by explaining the difference between the film *Oasis* and what his novel would look like. "Gong-ju, the protagonist, suffers from dementia. People don't feel good looking at her because she's ugly. It's hard to achieve this through writing. If you write this story, people will feel sympathy for her. But if they are confronted with an image of her, they will be disturbed. Through this, they will gradually accept the character, find her inner beauty and see her as a true human being. With a novel, this process would not happen. Words only reveal what they want to reveal." Lee is just inexhaustible on the specific relations between cinema and time: "The train in *Peppermint Candy* represents a journey through time. It is also the Lumière brothers' train in La Ciotat. Film is a medium that deals with time". However, Lee Chang-dong often returns to the film's relation to reality, which he sees as a difficult but essential relationship: "In my early days, I didn't want to be a director. But I was curious to know how films could be so remote from reality. So in my films, I wanted to reduce this distance between film and reality". Lee does not, however, have the Neo-Realists' unlimited trust in the uncovering of reality through film: «Making art is, in part, about turning one's back on reality. It is about wondering. It is not only about achieving a beautiful result but also about accepting the paradoxes of reality in all its complexity." And he adds, paraphrasing Godard in *Le Mépris* (who himself was distorting a sentence by Bazin): "Films are like dreams. They look like reality but they are not reality. For example, in dreams we express desires that we do not show in real life. The films correspond to our desires." If his films might be dreams, the irruption of fantasy into them is not without difficulty: "I had a difficult time shooting the scene with the elephant and the Hindu woman (*Oasis*). It was difficult to make a kind of fantasy realistic, and to make fantasy worse than reality, while using accessories that were usually meant for fantasy films." Lee Chang-dong, who can talk at length on the possible interpretations of his stories, places meaning at the center of his approach: "What is important (in a film) is that meaning is absent. Historically, meaning is the product of text (...). We are now at the age of post-meaning (...) film has become the dominant medium. The other media that dare to tackle meaning are weakened, degenerate, and have lost their power over people. Maybe because I come from literature, from text, I try to bring meaning into my films. »

Anyway, in the film world, Lee is best known as a demanding director of actors. He often explains: "For the direction of actors, I believe that the important thing is the human

43 ▶

factor. There are no rules. There are millions of ways of getting the best out of an actor. I often tell my actors to not act. I ask them to experience the emotions of the characters. I help them develop what they can feel by experiencing these emotions." And also: "I don't like the word «actor» (...). Being real and looking real are two different things. I have often had to resolve this conflict". In doing so, Lee confirms his special relationship with actors: "I didn't choose famous actors in my early days because I wasn't from the scene. I preferred young beginners. They have their own strengths. And the public does not yet have stereotypes about them." And he concludes: "I give a lot of freedom to the actors. They are in charge of developing characters who are open-ended questions for me."

44 ▶

DIALOGUE WITH LEE CHANG DONG*

Could we talk about your father? One constant element appears in your films: the father's absence. Moreover, this absence seems intentional. In *Burning*, the father appears very briefly for the first time in your filmography. It is a father who seems to want to convey his anger to his son. What was your relationship with your own father?

Before I talk about my father, I must make a few comments about the context of the period in which I was born. I was born on July 4 after the end of the Korean War, near the US base of the 8th USFK army in Daegu. My date of birth sounds like the title of Oliver Stone's film: Born on July 4th. When I was a kid, on my birthday, there was a fireworks display at night above the US Army base. Every time I went to see it, my older brother would say to me: "It's your birthday they're celebrating!". I really thought that the fireworks display was for me.

My father hated America. He was a failed socialist, like many intellectuals in Korea at the time. He refused to integrate into the capitalist superficiality of South Korean society, ruled by an anti-communist government. In other words, it meant that my father made no effort to earn money and support our family. As a result, it was my mother's role to ensure that we were fed. My mother gave brought up six children while earning money by making *hanboks* – traditional Korean costumes.

When I was a child, in my memory, my father was always drunk or angry. Sometimes both. He lived by destroying himself like a frustrated idealist. As a result, his family's life was also shattered. My father's anger was like a bomb, you never knew when he would explode. Everyone in the family feared my father. My mother was the most frightened of all. Although she was the only daughter of a good family, in keeping with Confucean tradition, she had never been to school. She never had a direct conversation with my father. Whenever she had something to tell him, she used us as intermediaries. For example, when we were all having dinner together, my mother would say: "Ask your father if he wants some more soup". Of course, you didn't have to ask for such a thing. If my father pushed his bowl of soup, it meant he still wanted some, and if he spat out: "I'm done!", that meant he didn't want any more soup. When we ate with my father, the whole family would fall into this heavy silence. That is why when I wrote novels and made films, I unconsciously avoided evoking the character of my father.

In your films, human suffering is remarkably under control. Do you think this reflects how you were affected by your experiences with your own family and childhood?

I don't think I can answer in the negative. These experiences from my childhood have affected me as a writer and a filmmaker. Tolstoy in *Anna Karenina* said that "happy families are all happy in the same way", while "unhappy families are each unhappy in their own way". But in my childhood, my house seemed to have inherited all kinds of pain. Within this immense panorama of pain, there is a multitude of colorful fabrics that were locked in a small room. I can still hear the sound of the sewing machine that covered everything. All of us six children ate and slept together in the small room; this room where my mother worked all day

* Conversations collected from October 2018 to June 2019 in Séoul.

sewing *hanboks*. At the heart of these dark memories is my sister who suffered from cerebral palsy. I cannot erase this from my memory. My sister, whose body was in constant torment, was the living proof of our misery. When a disabled person like her lives in a family, the whole family must share the consequences of this disability. But my sister was not ashamed of herself. She had trouble speaking, but she was relentless and always managed to join the conversation. She laughed often. And she also had her own code for laughter.

Your sister inspired, at least in part, the character of the disabled woman in the film *Oasis*. There are some optimistic and humorous aspects to this character.

The character of Han Gon-ju in the film wants to laugh all the time but, even in these humorous situations, she cannot help but feel a deep distress caused by her disability. She looks exactly like my sister. My family, who were poor, moved often. When we arrived in an unknown neighborhood, my sister became the target of the unhealthy curiosity of the local kids. Children then were more brutal than they are today. So when my sister went out, the children in the neighborhood followed her, calling her a moron: "Moron! Moron! Moron!" I had to fight these children. They called me the "moron's brother". My sister's presence isolated me. And in the narrow alleys of our poor neighborhood, there was a wall between me and the other children. It is in this context that I started writing all by myself. Maybe I needed to find my own way to communicate. When I was writing, I wanted to communicate with someone who was anonymous and invisible.

What kinds of stories did you write in your youth?

The first person who forced me to write was my mother. At the age of seven, when I was in elementary school, I learned to read and write. My mother forced me to write to my grandmother who lived in her hometown. She would dictate the letters. While she was sewing, she would tell me what I was supposed to write. And I did just that, lying down on top of pieces of fabric. They were clumsy letters: "Grandmother, are you feeling healthy in this hot weather? Thank you for worrying about us..." My mother thought that my letters could advantageously combine the innocence of a young boy with modesty, restraint and kindness. She knew very well the words that adults like to hear from the part of children. In that sense, my mother was a very creative person. I became famous for my letter writing among my relatives in my hometown. But I didn't feel like these letters were from me, even though I was writing them. I cheated the adults, stole their ways of complimenting. In a small room full of colorful clothes, our mother-son tandem secretly continued to write these letters. And gradually, I stopped enjoying the compliments I received for writing them, and started to feel ashamed of them. So I ended up writing my own letters. I realized it wasn't too difficult. I had already figured out what you are supposed to say to please the adults. Perhaps these first writings left their trace in me. Perhaps as a result of this first experience, I came to believe subconsciously that writing does not express something that comes out of me, a natural desire, but rather what the others expect and want to hear. Sometimes I still have doubts about myself. I ask myself if the films I make contain my most honest inner voice, whether they are not built according to the others' gaze and judgment.

When you were a child, did you feel like a storyteller?

When I was a child, I liked imagining stories. I knew a good friend who liked it when I told him my stories. I would talk and he would listen as we walked side by side. We called these walks «story walks». Sometimes one of my younger brothers came along. The walks took us out of our neighborhood into the heart of the city. The longer the story, the longer the route of our walk. When I was ten years old, I wrote a first story. It was the story of children who set out to rescue friends who had been kidnapped by a very bad adult. That's how I started writing. Writing became a kind of secret and deviant act, like masturbation, that no one in my entourage suspected for a long time.

If your first writing memories go back to the letters your mother forced you to write, what about your first film memories? Is there a moment in your life that you would call your first film experience?

When I was 12 years old, for the first time, an animated film was screened for the first time in South Korea cinemas. All the children knew about it and the film was very popular. My cousin knew I wanted to see it, and gave me some money to buy a ticket. So I ran there. But I felt strange when I saw the long line of children waiting in front of the entrance and the cash register. Suddenly, I thought it was a waste of money to spend it on this movie. Perhaps I wanted to leave the world of children. I left the line and went to another movie theater next door where *Lord Jim* (by Richard Brooks with Peter O'Toole) was showing. Of course I didn't know what kind of film that was, but I thought it was a film for adults and not children. This was the first film I chose by myself and for which I bought a ticket. I was too young to understand Lord Jim, but the story seemed to me as intense as a nightmare. A strange world at sea, in the storm, in the jungle and with strange foreigners. A few years later, I read Joseph Conrad's novel, which had been the inspiration for the film. And later still, I saw the film again and realized that my memory of the film was very different from what I was seeing then. But nevertheless, *Lord Jim*'s intense and bizarre images, and the fear and despair that I had found captivating during my childhood had stood the test of time. From that day on, cinema for me became a journey into the mystery that lies at the "heart of darkness", into the unknown lands that form our life.
I also participated in a film shoot. Kim Soo-yong shot his film *Sorrow Up in Heaven* at my elementary school when I about ten years old. The film was based on the true story of a student from the class next to mine. Japanese filmmaker Nagisa Oshima made a documentary on this film called *Diary of Yunbogi*. One Sunday, I went to my school where they were shooting. I was hoping to be able to play in the movie, even just as an extra. And I was lucky enough to be able to join the shoot. I was one of

45 ▶▶

children who ran out of the school under the rain. The film was a success, so much so that people used to say that all Koreans had seen it… but I didn't, because I couldn't afford a ticket. There were no copies of the film left, until a few years ago when a copy was found by chance in an archive in Taiwan. So thanks to a remastered version, I was able to see myself in the film! I walk in front of the camera for a few seconds with my umbrella under the rain (which was sprayed by a fire truck). It was even a tight shot!

Why did you choose to become a writer?

It is difficult to give a short answer.... It probably all begins with loneliness. As a child, I felt isolated. So I disappeared into my own world, a world of stories. So I wrote them down. I never showed them to anyone. But it was my way of communicating with someone who didn't have a face, someone I didn't know. When we were kids, there was the telephone game. You had to put a paper cup connected to a thread to your ear and pretend it was a phone. We imagined that the other person's voice would come through the phone. Writing, when I was young, was like this phone call. I would write imagining that I was communicating with someone. I still feel that way; my state of mind has not changed.

What were you like at twenty? In Murakami's *Barn Burning*, the narrator is a writer in his thirties, but in *Burning* he is only twenty. Why did you change that? To which extent is Jongsu like you?

Barn Burning is a short story in which the author claims to be the narrator. A writer in his thirties who lives a stable life, he talks to a young colleague in his twenties whose strange hobby is to burn barns in secret. But I thought that the protagonist should not be someone who has made it as a writer. Films whose main character is a writer are boring, aren't hey? *Burning* is a film about the ambiguity of the world we live in today. In the past, when I was young, the world's problems were simpler and more obvious. We knew what to fight against, whether it was to do with labor, capital or politics. But nowadays, it is more complicated and ambiguous. There's a problem and we can't figure out what it is. And yet this world appears sophisticated, comfortable, and apparently cool. To convey the mystery of this world, I thought I could follow the point of view of a young aspiring writer. He does not know yet what story he can write. He is desperate but powerless. And his rage is only burning deep inside him. He looks at the world around him and thinks about what he could write, and what meaning to give to his story. It's not much different from my experiences as a young twenty year-old writer. The problem is that I haven't really changed much, although I became a writer and I am now an old film director. I still have these same fundamental questions. What story, what movie? What is the meaning of the film I want to make? But no one is wondering about these things anymore...

At twenty, you were an aspiring writer and you played in the theatre. Why?

I have been close to the theatre since the age of ten because my brother, who was ten years older, started a stage career. This choice my brother made was one of my family's many misfortunes. There was almost no theatre in my hometown Daegu. Every time my brother put on a play, my mother had to get into debt with family and friends. Creditors would come to our house. I had to lie every time and say that my mother was not there. My brother would bring back actor buddies and they would rehearse in the room. I would sit in a corner and watch them play. Why was it so much fun for me? At a very young age, I learned to recite Hamlet's and Othello's monologues. «To Be or Not to Be, That's the Question..." My brother was sometimes Hamlet and at other times Iago. At that time, the only theatre in the city was on the station square. On the nights when one of my brother's plays was on, I always stood in front of the theatre watching people walk through this dark square. Most of them went to take a train, but some went to the theatre. I counted every one of them. I was afraid that not enough would come, and that we would be ruined again, and that the creditors would come back... When my brother was in the spotlight, I would stay in the shadows. After I finished high school, I started helping him. I distributed the flyers, glued the posters, worked as an extra, and finally started playing roles and directing plays. They were mostly Korean plays, but also sometimes plays by Peter Handke and Ionesco. So in my youth, I found myself somewhere in between literature and theatre. I was so happy when I was on stage that I was close to ecstasy, as if I was on drugs. But I thought I couldn't go on with theatre. I'd learned all the problems that it brought from looking at my brother. There couldn't be two theatre buffs in the house. I became a provincial high school teacher, left our town and the theatre behind, and became a writer.

How do you rate yourself as a writer?

I call myself a failed writer. When I took my first steps, a military regime was killing civilians who were demanding democracy in Gwangju, a large city in the southwest. And the whole nation was plagued by oppression and frustration. How could my sentences change reality? That question was always in my head. Adorno said: "You can't write poetry after Auschwitz anymore" but I was still obsessed with it. Literature should not deviate from reality and should stand by the suffering people. I was not alone, most writers of that period had to face this reality: it was becoming difficult to write. I was banging my head against the walls, but I couldn't write. The pleasure of writing comes from a free imagination. But that pleasure had evaporated and only the sense of duty remained. Anyway, when Korea moved to a democratic regime in the 1990s, the atmosphere rapidly changed. Writers were tired of books that tackled real issues, and everyone now talked about postmodernism, sensitiveness or everyday images. The only thing that had been democratized was the political institutions; but all the social issues we had been fighting for such a long time were now regarded as outdated, although they were still current. That was hard for me to accept. So I began to hate writing. I was a writer lost in this conversion of society. So I looked for a new way....

It could have been something other than cinema. How do you transform a writer into a filmmaker?

46 ▶

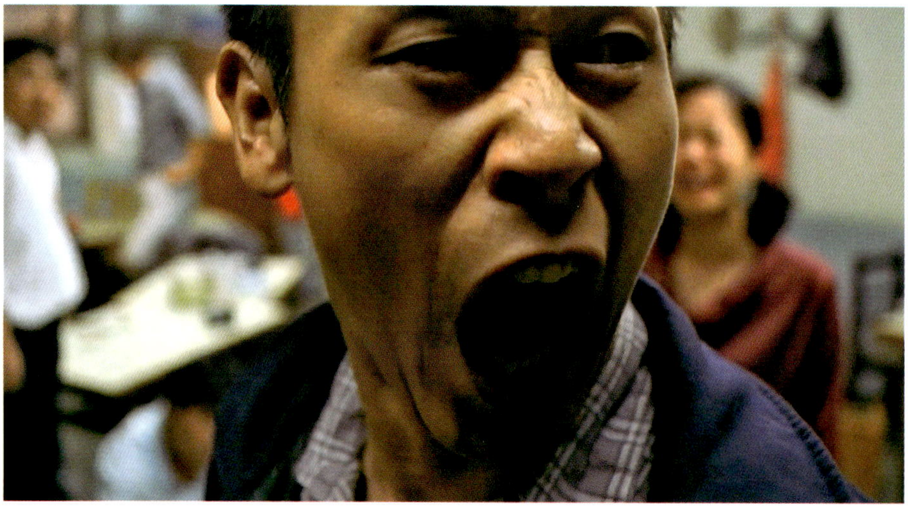

It's complicated. At that time, in Korea, when writers met, they talked about films and not about literature. Some even seriously considered making films. I remember a funny episode during a drunken evening. Some poet friends were drinking and talking about some films they had seen recently. And all of a sudden, I said I was going to make a movie. Of course, it was only a joke I had come up with to stop my friends from rambling on about those movies. I will make a film, I said, and I'll go to the Cannes Festival. I'll drive a white convertible from Paris to Cannes. I'll drive along the Mediterranean with *Follow Me* by Demis Roussos (which was the song that was playing in the bar at that moment) playing at full blast on my High Fidelity speakers, and you all will just have to follow me! My friends laughed at my teenage delusions. As you know, this joke became a reality a few years later. Except for the white convertible of course. But I really did think about moving to Paris with my family. A strange unrealistic project. I wanted to rent out our flat and spend a year or two in Paris with the money from the rent. Why this idea? It was for no reason. The imaginary Paris, the legendary Paris. The Paris that sheltered Hemingway and Fitzgerald. I asked director Park Kwang-su, who had studied cinema in Paris: how can I move to Paris? He said: life in Paris is expensive, and it helps to have student status. I didn't speak any French. What could I study? Cinema, Park Kwang-su told me, is the easiest subject you can study in Paris. All you have to do to study is watch movies in theatres. In Korea, at the time, it was difficult to see anything other than commercial Hollywood films. So I accepted Park's idea. He then advised me: there is no point in studying cinema with no preparation. You need to become familiar with film so that you get a feel for what is left for you to study. So he recommended that I get some field experience on film shoots in Korea. But I already felt too old for that. One day Park Kwang-su phoned me, asking me to introduce him to novelist Lim Chul-woo, whose novel *To the Starry Island* he wanted to adapt. Lim Chul-woo was a close friend. I had written a preface for his book. At the meeting with him and Park, I had an idea that Park liked and he asked me to write the script for the film. In exchange, I asked to be his assistant. That was our agreement. And I never went to Paris.

How was your screenwriting experience? What is the difference with novel writing?

When I write a novel, my text is mine, and no one can do it for me. But the script must, in any case, be written according to the wishes of the director. It was hard at first to accept that. When I was showing Park my script, he would make short comments: "Great!" or: "Boring!". I had to rewrite the bad passages. He would say "great" or "boring" without any further comment, without saying why. I had to think about it on my own. I felt frustrated, but very soon I realized that he himself did not know what the problem was. I understood that the director was someone who made requests to others without knowing what he himself expected! Anyway, what I had to try to understand was what was "great" and what was not from a cinematographic point of view. I learned a lot about film when I wrote my first script.

At that time, being an assistant director required for you to learn within a very strict system. How was your experience?

I wasn't an aspiring director. I never thought I would direct a movie one day. I wasn't either trying to gain some experience before going to Paris. In fact, I think that mostly I wanted to have a hard time. I was sick with myself, fed up with myself. It was like I was trying to punish myself for not having lived my life as I should and wasting my time. And in terms of punishment, my job as an assistant lived up to my expectations! It was a very hard job. *To the Starry Island* is a historical drama about the Korean War. It should have been a large-scale commercial film, but we created it in the spirit of independent films. The shooting took place on a small island in the south of Korea, and I worked much harder than everyone else. More than I was required to. I didn't even mind doing the most menial tasks, which were not part of the job of an assistant director. One day, a journalist came to interview me. I was roasting in the sun, my face had changed color, and I was preparing accessories for a fishing scene. The journalist announced to me that I had been chosen by his newspaper as the best young up-and-coming writer for the new millennium, and asked my what I was doing there while staring at me with astonishment. He was there to meet the writer of the new millennium and there I was, an assistant director. In his paper, he explained that I looked like a Hindu mystic who had mortified his body.

Your first film, *Green Fish*, is a gangster film, a film noir. Was it your intention to start with a genre film?

At that time, I was living in Ilsan, a suburb of Seoul. It was the first typical farming village in Korea to be transformed into a forest of apartment towers. And I was like a «new immigrant» there. I lived near Yeo Kyun-dong (a director) and Moon Sung-keun (an actor). We used to meet in coffee shops. We were thinking about Yeo's next movie. And I saw an old train station through the window. I said, as if I was talking to myself: "Where the hell are the people who used to live here? What are they doing today?" And my friend continued: "Imagine someone who has gone to the army and comes back here. How would they perceive all this change?" From this point on, I let my imagination run wild. We were just in the middle of a pause in a long discussion. "One day a man comes back from his military service (two years). He is on a train, he has opened the train's door to smoke a cigarette, standing on one of the steps. He sees a woman standing in the next door. And suddenly, the wind blows the woman's red scarf into the man's face. The woman he meets turns out to be a *femme fatale* who will change his destiny. Because she's the wife of a gang leader..." So I talked, playing around with the images of genre film. But Moon Sung-keun seriously encouraged me to write it up as a script. So I decided to write this story that felt within my reach, starting from the idea of a genre film. My idea was to draw the audience into a genre gangster movie, and then to take it into my own direction. After finishing the script, I didn't think it would become a

48 ▸▸

7

7

movie. I still didn't see myself as a director. The actor Han Suk-kyu was famous and all the scripts went to him, but he often refused them. I wanted to challenge myself and sent him my script. The next day, he called me to arrange a meeting. I realized it might be possible to make this film. Later, I learned that Han had been interested in the script because he was the last in a family of four children just like the character in the script called Mak-dong (which means "the youngest son"). I was lucky.

***Green Fish* depicts the nightlife in Yeongdeungpo as in a film noir, and the new city of Ilsan. This film introduces your relation to space, which you developed in later films.**

Yeongdeungpo and Ilsan are typical spaces and symbolic of Korea. When I was writing the script, I thought that this film should be a film about space. Yeongdeungpo is a night place, a stage for gangster, which encapsulates the country's economic development process. Ilsan is a new model for a type of city that can be seen everywhere now. One family, Mak-dong's, lives in Ilsan and the other, the gangsters' family, lives in Yeongdeungpo. The film shows an ironic comparison between a biological but divided family and a non-biological but very united gangster family. The young man is sacrificed for the benefit of this recomposed family. I wanted to show that the logic that prevailed in the mafia was similar to the mentality that had been ruling over South-Korean society for the past decades. Priority is given to fulfilling your objectives (*We can do it!*), without any regard how you get there. This mentality even justified the military dictatorship as a factor of economic development. This logic is also the reason why a city can suddenly emerge one morning. Ilsan and Yeongdeungpo are contrasting spaces like day and night in a film, but in the end they are both dominated by the same law of desire. The rapid changes in space also change the mind-set of Koreans. The main character is going through an identity crisis and keeps looking at himself in mirrors. Whenever he is about to do something decisive, he needs to know who he is and whether he really is himself.

Were you sure that the people who were familiar with the codes of genre cinema would follow you?

I hired Han Seok-kyu but I still had to work some more to secure all the funding. Investors had a problem that there was something different about my script, something different from other commercial films. At that time, the economic situation of Korean cinema was not good and the audiences were very small. The first screening of *Green Fish* was on a Saturday during the New Year's Eve break, which is supposed to be a great period for box-office. I was waiting outside the theatre when someone came to give me news from another local cinema. I was told that the cinema had had to cancel a screening of a Korean film that had come out a week earlier, after refunding the only two spectators that had turned up.

These were very hard times. It was not easy to venture into making your debut film as a director. As investors were not very confident in my talent as a director, I had to cut out some very personal elements in the film. But I couldn't give up the idea of hijacking a genre film in my own way. I wanted people to be unprepared for what happened in the story. It is a gangster movie but without a single action scene, without any revenge or catharsis. And what's more, after the main character dies, the film continues for another fifteen minutes! The protagonist's family opens a restaurant in this new city, which the mafia boss visits with his pregnant mistress. The family members serve them amiably without suspecting that these are the people who killed their son. I wanted the public to feel this terrible irony. I wanted to ask the public: what have we lost in order to obtain what we have now? This was my way of communicating with the public. I do not want to spoon-feed the public what they want.

You presented *Peppermint Candy* at the very beginning of the new millennium. Where did the inspiration come from?

Everyone was talking about the approach of the new millennium. Some scientists came on television to present their predictions on the future, which sounded like what was described in science-fiction books. I wanted to tackle the notion of time in a different way. To make a film where time would flow backwards. The idea came to me one morning as I was shaving. I looked back at my forty-something face in the mirror and sighed: "How I've changed! If only I could go back twenty years..." This was of course not possible in real life, but it can be in film. So I decided to make a film that would travel back in time, with a forty year old man going back to his twenties, his most beautiful and purest age, without using a time machine but cinematographically. *Peppermint Candy* came out on 1 January 2000 at midnight in South Korea. At the dawn of the new millennium, I wanted to question the public – and in particular, young Korean audiences – on the meaning of time. And that was twenty years ago already. How terrible!

Traditionally, a narrative tells a sequence of events in their chronological order. *Peppermint Candy* breaks this rule. How did this challenge and this adventure appear possible to you, after a first film that borrowed from the codes of genre cinema?

This was a mad challenge. At the time there had been some new films that challenged the codes of traditional Korean cinema, but *Peppermint Candy* was pushing this too far. After being turned down by a few celebrity actors including Han Suk-kayo, I made an even crazier decision: that of only hiring newcoming actors, which made things even more complicated. As I had not managed to secure funding from within the cinematographic industry, the actor Moon Sung-keun contacted a friend of his who was an exporter of leather goods. On the day we met, the guy asked me how much profit I believed the film would make. I said I would do all my best to ensure that he didn't lose more than 500,000 dollars. He laughed, as he probably wasn't expecting such a frank answer. And that was how I got the funding. The surprising thing is that the film did not lose any money. In retrospect, I think this was a period that saw the emergence of a new energy in the Korean film industry.

***Peppermint Candy* brings to mind *Citizen Kane's* "Rosebud" and is also reminiscent of this film's structure. Was this one of your references when you wrote the script?**

Citizen Kane is not the only film where a detail of daily life becomes an essential part of the whole story. In fact, at the time, I didn't have *Citizen Kane* in mind. When I was writing my screenplay, I was thinking more about the smell of Marcel Proust's madeleine and the idea of recovering time lost.

The film works its way back over twenty years, from 1999 to 1979. Over this period, Kim Yongho, the main character, experiences some crucial events in South Korea's modern history – including the financial crisis, the struggle for democracy or the Gwangju killings. Why did you decide that the final point of this time travel would be 1979?

Kim Yongho is an individual but he also stands for an ordinary Korean man who lived through the years 1979-1999. In 1979, Kim Yongho is twenty: the purest, most beautiful age. That was also the year of a new beginning and the return of hope for all Koreans. The dictator Park Chung-hee, who had been in power for twenty years, had just died, and we could now hope that the future would be different. People talked about the "Seoul Spring". But this spring was all too short. The army perpetrated the killings in Gwangju before taking over. Like all of us, Kim Yongho makes a series of choices, small or big, throughout his life. When he kills an innocent student in Gwangju, that is not his fault, he does not do it on purpose; but it is his personal choice to become a policeman and to cruelly reject Sunim. When they have committed a mistake, people can repent and try to lead a better life, but they sometimes make bad choices in order to avoid their feelings of guilt, which is stupid. Yongho also suffers from guilt, he believes that he is a murderer who is not worthy of the love of Sunim, a kind and pure woman, and he lets her go in the most merciless way. At the time, the Koreans had just had as a President of the Republic the chief of the army that had killed innocent civilians in Gwangju. Chun Doo-hwan was elected by his fellow countrymen, although this was an indirect vote that took place when the press was under control. I wanted to convey to the spectators the meaning of the choices we make in the innumerable moments of our existence.

You talk about cruel irony at the end of *Green Fish*, but *Peppermint Candy* truly reveals the irony of life. Is this sense of irony a crucial element in your cinema?

It is, yes. It is the very nature of life. Travelling back in time enabled me to show the irony of time and life. For instance, Yongho hates dogs and often kicks them. But years later (so towards the beginning of the film) when he visits his daughter and ex-wife, she doesn't open the door and the dog is the only one that expresses joy at seeing him and shakes its tail. If you go back in time, that is if you reverse cause and effect and look at elements whose consequences you already know, you truly feel how ironic our life is. They say that the Ancient Greeks had two concepts of time: on the one hand, time that can be broken down into even units like seconds or minutes; on the other, time as it is remembered upon the approach of death,

and whose weight and meaning can feel different. *Peppermint Candy* is a film about asking yourself about the meaning of the time you have experienced, before you die.

In *Peppermint Candy*, did you shoot the sequences in the reverse order of the story, or according to its original chronology? What motivated this choice? The film is divided into seven chapters. Did you clearly set them apart to shoot them?

I had to shoot the seven chapters independently and separately, because each chapter comes at a different time. The protagonist had a different hairstyle and even a different weight. So it was as if the film was actually made up of seven short films. We shot in the final order of the film. This shooting order was not only due to technical conditions, it was also a crucial problem. A story has a cause/effect structure. The idea was that the more the narrative arc developed, the more the emotional arc grew until it reached what is called *climax*: the culminant point that results from the conjunction of these two arcs. In this film, the causal structure is top-down and as both arcs evolve, events become simpler and simpler. As the film progresses, the main question becomes the intensification of emotions, even though the events have become simpler. Here is the important point: the narrative structure is disrupted but the emotional progression must continue to grow. It is a very good idea to shoot a film in the order of the story's progression, so actors can capitalize on the various experiences and feelings related to the events. But in our case, we had to go back in time while experiencing emotions. The more information your hold back, the more emotion you gain. This was the opposite of what is usually done in film, but it was an intense and very special experience for the actor. In fact, Sol Kyung-gu shot six chapters and when he realized what his character's hidden trauma was, he cried spontaneously. The scene we shot was the one where the actor could not hold back his emotions, but he could not do it again a second time.

The train and the camera play a major part in the film. Were they important elements to express the meaning of time?

These are important elements to communicate the topic of time. The camera captures moments. Printing film onto paper means preserving the time that it contains. In the film, when Yongho sells his camera, the shop owner gives back to him the film that was in the camera. Spectators then think that what is on this film will play a role in the story, but in the next scene Yongho exposes the film to the sun. Time captured on film is destroyed and vanishes if it is not printed. That was what I wanted to show. In addition, at each new chapter, we see a train rolling back to the past. This train also appears at decisive times in Yongho's life. This is how time is made visible. The train is a symbol of modernity. It has transformed human notions of time and speed. Modern technology invented cinema, one of the first films by the Lumière brothers was called *The Arrival of a train in the station of La Ciotat*. For me this is very symbolic.

***Oasis* is a love story with a touch of fantasy. But the film does not follow the usual template of romantic films, nor does it create fantasy in the**

way we usually see in film. How did the idea for this film come about?

I had just gone to the Cannes Film Festival for the first time for *Peppermint Candy*. At first I didn't feel comfortable in this atmosphere. There were too many people! The red carpet that rises to the sky, the incredible flashes of the photographers, the immense sun and the bewitching blue sea... All this plunged me into an unreal world. In front of the crowd on the façade of the Palais des Festivals, there was a film poster that said "Better than sex". I thought: everyone sells fantasies. I stood there for a moment in the middle of the crowd. I was thinking about cinema as a form of fantasy, and I decided to make a film about fantasies.

For you, is a film about fantasies necessarily a love story?

Love is for two and fantasy is for two. For others, it could look like masturbation or crime. This film is a romance between two people. A love that cannot be accepted as love. A love between two people we tend to want to look away from in real life. I wanted to know how the public would accept the consequences of their own fantasies. This is certainly not the type of fantasy that a spectator would expect from a film. A «normal» love story is about an attractive man and woman who live a fulfilling and moving love, satisfying the public's fantasies. But the fantasy in this film is so petty and ugly and realistic that it becomes unacceptable. In the film, the oasis appears in the background of a naive tapestry. I thought the film was about this boundary. The boundary between reality and fantasy, between film and reality, between disabled and non-disabled. Anyway, the film was a comfortable success in Korea. When I spoke with members of the audience who told me that they had been touched by the love story between the two protagonists, I wondered about the nature of this emotion.

For *Oasis*, you used a hand-held camera for the first time. Was it to break the "fantasy" element of the film?

In this film, I used a hand-held camera from beginning to end. I clearly wanted to break the frame. From the Renaissance, when paintings were framed, each frame symbolized a perfect aesthetic world. The painting became detached from the rest of the world and inward facing. Frame in a film is the same thing. It creates the impression that the world off-camera doesn't exist. I wanted the public to feel this limit (almost unconsciously) by constantly challenging the framing. This also meant challenging the boundary between film and reality. I also placed a shooting scene to remind the public that they are in a movie. The main character, Jongdu, drives a Chinese restaurant delivery motorcycle at night and goes to the Han Gongju's house. On his way back, he sees the dolly tracks, accidentally stumbles onto the set and disrupts the shooting. Then he shouts at the crew to ask who is playing in this film.

After *Oasis* you were nominated Minister of Culture. The news was surprising. How did this happen?

That year, 2003, after turbulent elections, Roh Moo-hyun, a progressive president from a minority background, was elected. The

50 ▶

president had promised not to appoint a politician but someone from the art world, and he solicited me (unfortunately!). There were many reasons, but perhaps the main one was to defend the film quota system. By complete chance, I found myself at the frontline to negotiate the quota battle against the United States. At first, I refused the post. But in the end, I could not avoid accepting this bitter appointment.

You have been compared to the writer André Malraux, who was also a Minister of Culture in France. What do you think of that?

Comparing me to Malraux is an honor, but it is too much. As you know, he was part of this contemporary period when the spirit of the French Resistance was an essential part of the Republic. In his time, many French people supported his ambitious vision. But when I became a minister, I was the object of harsh criticism from politicians and the conservative press. They spent their time judging me and attacking me. Nevertheless, I tried to firmly establish the principle according to which, although the government supports the arts, there should be no political interference in them. During my time as a minister, I tried to influence Korea's policies for the arts and to deliver political measures with adequate resources that were designed to last for several decades. In this sense I can say that I worked in keeping with André Malraux's spirit.

Your first film after resigning as minister was *Secret Sunshine* (Korean title: *Miryang City*). In this film, as in your previous films, the space, the city of Miryang, is important. Why did you choose this city as a backdrop for this film? Do you have a special relationship with Miryang?

Myriang is a small town at an hour's drive from Daegu, my hometown. I remember going there with my college girlfriend: we stayed by the river, and the sunlight was very pleasant. It is a typical Korean small town. A small town from which the beauty and peace of the past have disappeared, giving way to materialism. Anyway, the name of the city sounded very poetic to me. If you translate the Chinese characters, *Miryang* means "full sun", but this name can also be interpreted as "secret sun". I thought it was symbolic – an ordinary and materialist town with such a poetic name. I thought it symbolized our life. Since I had been making films, I had wanted to shoot in Miryang. So I did eventually. The film was entirely shot in Miryang, except for one or two places, like the prison. The places in Miryang were decisive. Not for its cinematographic aspects, but because it is so banal, uninteresting and ordinary. It was about questioning the ordinary routine and banality of life.

In this daily life, however, the female character Shin-Ae suffers enormously. Is this the irony of life?

Unexpected pain happens every day, that's life. No one escapes pain. It is also a human desire to experience pain. Humans also have this desire to suffer. The more desire you feel, the greater the suffering. So Shin-Ae, who was betrayed by her husband, returns to his hometown to deny the evidence of his treason. She tries to recreate the story of this betrayed love but she is faced with tragedy.

Because she does not want to be ignored by her neighbors, she claims to have money and to want to invest this money in buying land. Because of this, she will lose her son. This is all paradoxical. She is destroyed by this excess of foolish desires, like Oedipus. Shin-Ae is the bravest and at the same time one of the most stupid of my films' characters. She is a woman who fights God. Like a mythological hero. The greatest irony is in forgiveness. She thinks she'll be saved by forgiving her son's killer. But this will lead her to greater despair. Is it possible to forgive? Can God forgive the sins of men? What kind of God would he be? These are very difficult questions.

With respect to the theme of forgiveness, it has been said that *Miryang* was full of references to Korea's political context. Is this the case?

The film is based on Yi Chong-joon's short story «Worm Story», which was published in a literary magazine in the late 1980s. At that time, the backdrop was the struggle for democracy and the Gwangju massacre of 1980. The themes of forgiveness and reconciliation were in vogue in political circles and in the media. There is no mention of Gwangju in the story, but as I read it, I felt that there was a lot of anger because of the fact that the victims had been excluded from discussions about forgiveness and reconciliation,. If the offender is a collective entity like a state, the question of forgiveness is always a political one. This is especially true for Koreans who lived through the Japanese colonial era, the Korean War and the military dictatorship. In any case, in *Miryang* the character's suffering seems to me to go beyond the category of «victims». It is close to the existential and fundamental suffering of man. It is not attributed to the criminal but to God.

The actors in your films often seem like they are pushing their limits. This is particularly visible in *Oasis*. Do you have a specific method for directing actors?

Maybe a million, which means none at all. I often ask my actors not to act but to be true. They often find this puzzling: "Wait, I'm an actor, so what does it mean if I am not acting?". I tell them to not try to express a feeling, but to just feel the character. Of course, it is never as simple as just saying it. This sometimes requires lengthy discussions with my actors. We talk about our own experiences, not just about the movie. It's already in Stanislavski's method. Actors can express extreme feelings that they have never lived through, by digging through their experiences. I call this: "holding the door handle". Even if the door is very heavy, you can open it by using the handle. The director must help the actors hold the handle. What more can they do? In *Oasis* Moon Sori was to interpret a mentally handicapped person. This required a lot of intense physical effort, so much so that we had to have a masseuse on the set. She had to twist her body while expressing subtle inner feelings. No other actor could have done more than her. First of all, actresses hate to mess up their body's image, to a point that we cannot imagine. Moon went beyond that. Jeon Do-yeon, who plays the role of Shin-Ae, also had difficulties with her role. At the time, she was already a star with a great acting technique. I asked her to feel Shin-ae's character without expressing it. To "feel" events (the kidnapping and death of her son, the loss of her faith, etc.) instead of expressing them meant taking on this boundless pain. She said that each day of shooting she asked herself if she would make it. She never thought that the pain caused by a single event could continue to grow every day. The most difficult for her was that the director never told her how to express this concretely. She ended up hating me. Shin-Ae hates God, but it's hard to hate something that's invisible. Her hatred of the director took the place of her character's hatred of God. Of course, after the shooting, the hatred disappeared. She finally understood me and won an award in Cannes. Jeon and Moon's performances are impressive, but the male supporting actors Song Kang-ho and Sol Kyun-gu are also excellent. Their acting is not externalized but it really lives on film, and it balances the whole film out.

***Miryang* seems to question the spectators about the visible and the invisible. The sun is visible on screen but God is invisible.**

It is a religious issue and, at the same time, a cinematographic issue. How can the film transmit what is invisible to the viewer? And how can the visible be communicated? To disrupt religious activities, Shin-Ae plays the song «This is a lie» on a loud speaker and shouts at the pastor that his sermon is a lie. This reveals her desperate feeling of being betrayed by God and, at the same time, it shows her entering into a clinical phase of paranoia and megalomania. The important thing is that this act does not deny the existence of God. To fight God is to recognize his existence. But fighting God is also called insanity. What is the difference? What I want to emphasize is that the film is not about religions or God, but about people.

At the end, Shin-Ae looks at herself in a mirror to cut her hair. Jongchang (the main actor) takes the mirror from her. What does that mean?

It means: "Look at yourself! Salvation is also in you." Where can Shin-Ae find a reason and the strength to live? By cutting her hair with her own strength and hands. I don't know if there are any leads to follow with this. She has always been in search of Heaven and of the meaning of life. But the meaning of life does not come from high above. Alongside her is Jongchan who looks very banal, and a ray of sun over a messy garden. What she needed most was to face herself, to accept herself. Facing oneself requires more courage than facing God. After leaving the hair salon with her hair half cut, she meets the owner of a clothing store who says to Shin-ae: "You're crazy! You're leaving after only having half of your hair cut!" And they both burst out laughing. She looks at herself in the mirror and finishes cutting her own hair. From the moment she realizes she might have gone crazy, she resumes her life. My film is a story of awareness. Our stupid ambitions chase the Holy Grail, which can never be found. But we gain awareness along the way, even if we never reach our goal.

How did you create the movie *Poetry*?

While I was writing the script for *Miryang*, there was this case in Miryang where a

53 ▶

young girl had been raped by a group of boys. This idea stayed with me during the whole shoot. I wanted to tell this story in a film, but I didn't know how to do it. At first, I thought of Raymond Carver's short story, "So Much Water So Close To Home", but I thought the plot felt too familiar. During a stay in Kyoto, Japan, while reading Kundera in front of the TV in my hotel, I had an idea. It was supposed to be a TV program for travellers who couldn't sleep. Meditation music floating over peaceful and beautiful landscapes. There was a peaceful river, flying birds and fishermen with nets. As I was looking at the screen, the idea of the title came to me: it had to be a cruel story, and the title had to be *Poetry*. And would be the story of an old lady in her 60s who was writing for the first time in her life. It didn't come from logic or thought, but it emerged instinctively and intuitively. My travelling companion was an old friend, a poet. When I told him about my idea, he was not convinced about this project: "Who will want to see a film about poetry?" he asked me. He also recommended that I did not let the success of my films (even if it was small) go to my head. Strangely enough, this convinced me even more to make the film. Why a film about poetry? Because it is time for poetry to die. "So poetry deserves to die!" said my friend. I promised to keep this sentence in my film.

The protagonist Mija tries to write poetry for the first time in her life but at the same time, she gradually loses her mind because of Alzheimer's disease. This story is also full of irony.

This film is the story of an adventure. It is a surprising and wild adventure, like seeking the Holy Grail of poetry. At the same time, she loses the memory of words, which reveals life's cruel paradox and irony. Of course, memory loss is also a symbol of death. Forgetting is a form of death. This makes his adventure more tragic. But she eventually makes it through. The irony of life is that you have to lose something to get something else. I also write poetry. Writing poetry also means discovering beauty. But beauty does not exist only in beauty alone. As night exists only with light, beauty exists with dirt, ugliness and pain.

Why did you choose the actress Yun Jung-hee? How did this collaboration go?

The first time I thought about this character, in my hotel room in Kyoto, I wrote that she would look like "a young girl at a picnic, a hat on her head and a colored scarf around her neck". The fact that she looked like a young girl despite her real age was a key description of her character. Even as an older woman, she keeps this intimate characteristic. And Yun Jung-hee is this kind of person. When I thought about Mija, I thought about her. I did not know her personally, although we had already met in film festivals. But I had this instinctive conviction that she was like the character. Yun Jung-hee was a legendary Korean actress. After playing in almost three hundred films in the sixties and seventies, she had retired from film after she married pianist Baek Kun-woo and she was living in Paris. In my teens, Yun was a shiny star in the sky rather than a terrestrial creature. How could I have imagined I would one day work with her? Before I started writing the script, I had dinner with her and I told her the story. I had no need to convince her: she was very interested in the story. The name Mija is old-fashioned. In Chinese characters, it means "the beautiful thing", and it actually is her real name. That was a pure coincidence, contrary to what she thought, I did not know her real first name. Yun is an inspired and expressive actress. Although she had shot many films in her youth, live sound recording was a new experience for her. At the time, post-recorded sound was meant to emphasize expressions. So if I asked her to not express but to feel, this was not easy for her to understand. Eventually, she completely understood the way I worked, even better than the younger actors in the film. She lived in the film as herself.

***Poetry* questions beauty and life. Do you think that the spectators will find answers there?**

I don't like movies that give me answers. Movies that force their message. Commercial films have the most obvious messages. Justice must win, or should win. But that is a simplistic and not very interesting message. All important works of art ask a question. In *Poetry*, the problem is to find the link between true beauty, ethics and human morality. I have always asked myself this fundamental question as an artist, ever since the beginning of my career. In other words, what work of art can I create to fight against the absolute misery and evil of this world? How can I find true beauty? I ask the questions to the public, and I hope they find answers. The meaning of the film's ending is also in the minds of the audience. I don't want a film that the audience forget as soon as they walk out of the theatre. I want the film to be connected to the minds of the audience, to their lives.

In the film, the poet says that it is important to see well. Is this something you believe?

Yes, I think that good poetry reaches beyond reality as we see it, beyond the visible world. It is not about getting rid of reality and of the world, but rather about getting into it. How can we see the world? This is an essential question for making poetry and films. The film shows the world as a substitute for the eyes of the audience. Through what gaze do we show the world in our films? Some films show the world in a new way. Other films only show what you want to see. And other films don't see anything at all.

This film has an open ending. The end of the story belongs to the audience, just like reading certain poems. Was this ending your intention?

At the end of the film, Mija manages to write a poem. But this is not enough. She must make «choices». In this sense, the film is about her «choices». Will she report her grandson to the police? The choice is not clearly shown in the film, it remains a possibility. It is up to the public to fill this void. And finally, she disappears. Where has she gone? The destinies of the schoolteacher and the girl seem to overlap, but I wanted to leave the audience free to interpret these destinies. Her last poem is entitled: "Songs of Agnes". It is her only poem left in the world and it talks about the girl, Agnes. This is the voice that this girl wanted to leave in the world. One person's song replaces

◀ 54

◀ 55

another person's story. I think that this is what artists do.

Burning came eight years after _Poetry_. What did you do all this time?

I taught my students in college, and I produced films by young directors. But I could not make my own films. I was asking myself questions. What film could I make? And what could I say through a film? I prepared many projects, and I wrote up three of them. But I did not do anything because I couldn't find any answers to my questions. "Is this really necessary?" I couldn't start a story without wondering if it was necessary to do it, even if people thought the idea was interesting. I could not commit if I was not fully convinced. I think this problem only gets worse for me. Which film will convince me? I cannot explain this logically. It is just a feeling I cannot explain. This deranged obsession with perfection. There were many stories of angry individuals in my batch of projects in preparation. People today seem angry all over the world, regardless of nationality, religion or social class. I thought that young people's anger was a specific problem. I decided to do *Burning* because it was about the rage of youth.

Haruki Murakami's short novel, _Barn Burning_, has a mysterious ending. How do you relate this to the idea of rage?

Murakami's story tells a little mystery about an unknown young man who burns barns. And the ambiguity remains until the end. I thought that this ambiguous ending could be related to the world we live in today and to the ambiguity of our lives. The world is becoming more and more elegant, comfortable and beautiful. But personal lives are getting smaller and more mediocre. In the past, I had the impression that the world could improve and that history was progressing. But nowadays, young people no longer have this faith and hope. There's fewer jobs are lacking, rents are rising and economic inequalities are increasing. Strangely enough, it seems that this is not a problem on the surface. Inequalities are also becoming more sophisticated. Young people know that something is wrong, but they don't know what to do or what to fight. For them, I feel that the world is this monstrous mystery, like in the movie where Ben could be a serial killer or a sweet and kind friend. And so they feel desperate and they burn inside. In fact, the first person who told me about this story was Oh Jung-mi, the scriptwriter I had been working with for five years. She told me that she felt this rage when she read about these "completely useless" barns that became vinyl greenhouses in the film. What if it had been people who were declared "useless" instead of barns? She explained that the idea of judging someone as useless and getting rid of them was frightening and enraging. This idea resonated with the notion of «useless persons». Young people are afraid of being categorized as «useless». So, on this huge treadmill called «social competition», they have to run without ever stopping.

Burning is based on a story by Murakami, but you believe it is an evocation of Faulkner's world: in what sense?

The interesting thing is that there is a story by Faulkner that has the same title as Murakami's story. I don't think this is a coincidence. Faulkner's story is about a poor farmer and his young son who secretly burn down a barn out of anger. As you know, Faulkner wrote about the difficult lives of the poor living by the Mississippi. He stated at the Nobel Prize ceremony that it was the duty of an author to write about the souls of those who suffer all their lives. Murakami writes differently. He deviates from the seriousness of reality and crosses the border between reality and a fantasy world inhabited by a light and boundless imagination. This seems to be his strength as a writer who fascinates audiences in both the West and the East. The two writers are on two different sides of the story. If Faulkner's barn is the object of a rage that is born out of pain, Murakami's barn is the object of a strange hobby. Maybe it not a real object but rather a product of the imagination or a metaphor. Even if the film is inspired by Murakami's short story, it is linked to Faulkner's world and to real suffering, rage and guilt. In other words, it is the story of young Faulkner living in the world of Murakami. Like Faulkner's protagonist who feels guilty and frightened because of his father, Jongsu, the young man in the film, looks at today's sleek and postmodern world with anguish and rage inherited from his father. We no longer live in Faulkner's world. Literature is not taken as seriously by writers and readers anymore. In *Burning*, Jongsu tells Ben that Faulkner is his favorite author and that his stories are similar to his life. Ben answers that all this is too serious: "Seriousness is not fun". That is what producers, viewers and other directors tell me: "Your films are too serious. They're not fun!" They think that this way of dealing with reality and the world in which we live, of approaching our existence seriously, is old-fashioned. They think that ignoring all this is cool, casual and sophisticated.

The mystery in *Burning* seen as a thriller seems to rest upon the ambiguity of Ben's character. How did you build this character when you worked on the script with your scriptwriter?

The film is about the mystery of today's world. Jongsu says to Ben: «I think the world is a mystery». And for him, this mystery is Ben. If he kills him at the end – and it's not certain that it actually happens, as it may happen in the book that he's writing – it is not because Jongsu believes that Ben is a serial killer but because he can't figure out who he is. This mystery about his identity makes him angry. The research on this character was the main challenge of the script. My screenwriter Ho Jung-mi studied Russian literature. She translated a book by Mikhail Lermontov entitled *A Hero of Our Time*, where he writes about new kind of evil. Ben looks like the psychopaths you see in movies, but he can also be very different. He may be a sweet, innocent young man who has enough money to do what he likes, but who feels empty inside, dissatisfied, like many young people in today's capitalist society. It may not even matter if he really is a serial killer. We don't know what he has done to be so rich, but he says that what he does is "not unlike games". In fact, many professions are like that nowadays. Professionals sit

56 ▶

comfortably at home, tapping on their keyboards, and make huge profits. In a few clicks, they can fire hundreds or thousands of workers. They can take the lives of millions of people who know neither their names nor their faces, without their hands ever being covered in blood. But these people also say that this is "the morals of nature". It is like a flood that lets the bodies float at the surface. It represents the logic of capitalism, which mimics the voice of God. They enjoy an incredible abundance but their heart is empty like that of a psychopath. It is similar to Nietzsche's "last man" in *Thus spoke Zarathustra*. It is the image of today's pure Evil.

How did you work with the actor to preserve this character's mystery and ambiguity until the end?

Steven Yeun, who plays Ben, understood the character from the beginning. In fact, it was difficult to describe Ben logically. If an actor had told me when reading the script that he didn't understand Ben's character, I wouldn't have taken him in the cast. In reality, there were two potential actors. But when I met Steven in Seoul, I felt that he understood the character not logically but inside his body. He said that this man had this "emptiness" at his core. He added that he knew this because he had experienced it. He spoke of his existential crisis, which he experienced as an obscure Asian actor who experienced sudden fame and wealth. I understood that he was getting at the heart of Ben's character. A modern vacuum, materially wealthy and super-powerful, but which can do nothing. To play Ben, you had to start from an inner void, whether he was a young man full of money or a serial killer psychopath, who burns people like useless greenhouses. Anyway, Ben had to remain mysterious until the end. How well should an actor know himself? Each actor must have an inner motivation to play each scene, even to express small details. I have talked a lot to Steven about this problem and tried to balance the ambiguity in small details. It was also to maintain the tension throughout the film and maintain a high level of intensity, like walking on a tight rope. I didn't have to agree with him as to whether he should play a serial killer or not. I asked him at the very end of the shooting when he passed in front of me by chance, if his character was a killer. He replied: "I won't answer. I'm the only one who should know." And he burst out laughing.

The scene where Haemi (the young female protagonist) dances is a truly cinematographic scene. How was this scene prepared?

It was when I imagined this scene and the one at the end that I knew I could write the script. These images were catalysts for me to make this film. Haemi's dance scene is at the heart of the film and had to be perceived as a mystery. It happened at dusk, a moment when the limit of light and day is reversed. Real and unreal, ugly and beautiful, happy and unhapy, etc. The beautiful sunset, the floating flags, Miles Davis' notes, the mooing calves, the messy wasteland. Despite all these elements, this had to be perceived as a mystery. The most important thing was freedom. Haemi dances her feeling of freedom. Like Bushmen from the Kalahari Desert. I wanted the audience to feel what would come from a very distant past, from the origin. With the director of photography, we prepared the scene so that it would not be too artificial, and that so that it could capture something spontaneous. Haemi's dance was, in fact, very prepared and we worked on the choreography for a long time. But when we were shooting in front of the camera, we let things go freely. Everything was planned, as always, but I wanted to be open to surprises. In any case, the result was fortuitous and not what we expected with all our efforts and calculations.

In this scene, we hear Miles Davis' music, well known for its use in *Elevator to the Gallows* by Louis Malle. Was this music an inspiration to you? In *Burning*, the music's role is to accelerate the suspense. But in general, you refrain from using music in the soundtracks of your movies – to the point that no music is used at all in *Poetry*. What role does music play for you?

As you said, I prefer not to use music in my movies. Music artificially reinforces emotion. Paying attention to this was particularly important in *Poetry*, which is a film about the search for true beauty. I wanted to show what it could be without artificial beauty. People can hear music in their daily environment with the sound of rain or the cries of children. Actually, there's too much music in movies. But the best thing would be for the audience to feel the musicality of a scene without any music. When I shoot or set up a scene, I always look for its musicality. In the specific case of *Burning*, I liked Mile Davis' music, especially in *Elevator to the Scaffold*. And above all, this track seemed to create a threatening and invisible tension in the film.

Sartre asked Flaubert (post-mortem): "Why did Madame Bovary have to die in the end?" In the same way, I would like ask you why does Ben have to die at the end of *Burning*?

This question is like asking: why does Jong-su have to kill? And it is also a question of how you interpret the final scene. I thought the film was geared towards this ending. As if that was an inevitable consequence. Because *Burning* is, once again, a story of rage. The rage that the main character tries to keep in him and that eventually explodes. As I said before, this rage stems from the ambiguity of the world. And this scene has a second part, a second fear. In fact, the film seems to be about trying to unravel Ben's mystery, but I wanted to leave the question in the hands of the audience and in Jongsu's: "Who is Jongsu?". I wanted his naked body in the final scene, like a newborn baby, shaking with fear and sadness, and with unknown feelings that could be delivered as a cinematographic question. What will happen to Jongsu now? What will he do in the future? This is related to the novel he is writing. What novel is he going to write about this mysterious world? The question is also: what story does he or do we want? These questions are necessarily moral, ethical, political, social and perhaps also the product of a purely cinematographic imagination.

This sort of mystery/thriller movie also explores political and economic issues. One could also say that it depicts the process of the creation of a novel. Finally, you seem to question the public about the story: what story did you expect to discover? Is it telling the truth?

Today, cinema tries to give the public an immediate "experience" – whether that's in space, in a World War Two battle or in a murder scene, the public can live this scene as if they were there. Over time, cinema is becoming simple and easy. The simple narrative of a super-hero who saves the world captivates the public. The world is becoming increasingly complex so why is cinema simplifying it? Think about the Marvel films with their super heroes who save the world. Recently in Korea, *Avengers* was shown in up 90% of cinemas. It swept every other film away like a tsunami. In Antiquity, the Greeks rejoiced in the tragedies of heroes fighting their own fate, producing a revelation of life through catharsis. Today, we are enthusiastic about superheroes who save the world with their superpowers. 2,000 years have passed since Sophocles. What has happened to humanity during these 2,000 years? *Burning* is struggling to reverse the trend of current films. I don't give simple and easy answers, but I open up questions. Is Ben a serial killer or a generous rich friend? Where did the woman go? And I wanted these questions to extend to the film itself and to question cinema. How close it is to the truth, to what I see and believe in? What level of truth about life and the world is achieved by the films I watch? What story do I want? And ultimately, what is a film? I wanted to offer a new and exciting cinematographic experience where people naturally come out with questions.

Do you believe in the public's intelligence?

I would like to say that I don't make films with the public's intelligence in mind. But I make films to communicate with the public whoever they are. Maybe it is my own way of doing things, perhaps a bit demanding. I set up obstacles, like in a race where they have to be overcome. But I create these obstacles thinking of the joy of meeting the people who have overcome these obstacles.

57 ▶▶

BIOGRAPHY

Lee Chang-dong was born in 1954 in Daegu in the province of Gyeongsang, in a left-wing family with roots in the Korean aristocracy. An introverted child, he started writing historical stories from an early age. As his older brother was a theatre actor in his hometown, Lee soon got into theatre and acted in a few plays. In 1980, after his education studies degree at Kyungpook university, he started teaching in a provincial high school. His first novel *Jeon-ri* received an award from newspaper *Dong-a*. He was transferred to a high school in Seoul where he got involved with the theatre scene, while also continuing to write. He published two collections of short stories, *So-ji* and *There is a Lot of Shit in Nok-Cheon*, which were acclaimed by the literary establishment. In 1992 director Park Kwang-su, whom he had met in 1988 at the première of *Chilsu and Mansu*, the film that inaugurated the Korean New Wave, commissions him to write an adaptation of the novel *To the Starry Island*. In 1993, he became his assistant for the shooting of the film. In 1995 he wrote another screenplay for Park Kwang-su, *A Single Spark*, on the life and sacrifice of union leader Chun Tae-il. He lost several novels in progress when his computer crashed, including a biography of a famous South Korean CEO.

A friend of his, the actor Myung Kae-nam, founded production company East Film in 1996 and decided to produce Lee Chang-dong's first film, *Green Fish*: the story of an ordinary man who finds himself involved with the local mafia. His directing career took off, with a cast of celebrities he would never have dreamt of bringing together: Han Seok-kyu, Moon Seung-keun and Shim Hye-jin. The film was awarded in local and international festivals (Vancouver, Rotterdam). Lee Chang-dong immediately acquired a reputation as an implacable and demanding director of actors, which intensified with the filming of *Peppermint Candy*, the story of an ordinary Korean man told backwards (which received awards at the Bratislava and Karlovy Vary festivals), and *Oasis*, featuring the actress Moon So-ri (Silver Lion at the Venice festival) who plays a disabled woman. Lee became a teacher at the new National Korean Film School (KNUA), where his colleagues included Park Kwang-su as well as Hong Sang-soo who was teaching screenwriting there.

In 2002, Lee Chang-dong became more active politically. He supported the campaign of Roh Moon-yong, the democrat candidate to the Presidency, who had been the lawyer of opponents to the dictatorship in the 1980s. When Roh was elected, he nominated Lee Chang-dong in the post of Minister of the Arts and Culture because he did not want a politician in this position but a professional. Lee Chang-dong first refused before eventually accepting the offer, but the battle over screen quota caused him to resign after a year. In 2006, Lee received the French Légion of Honor.

In 2007 he returned to cinema with *Secret Sunshine*, which was selected for the Cannes Film Festival. The main actress Jeon Do-yeon, playing a young widow who returns to her husband's provincial hometown and goes through an existential crisis after her son's murder, receives the Cannes award for best actress. Like *Oasis*, *Secret Sunshine* was nominated for best foreign language film at the Academy Awards. In 2010, Lee Chang-dong directed *Poetry*, the story of a woman in her sixties with a passion for poetry who has to deal with Alzheimer's disease and with an out-of-control grandson. The film received the award for best screenplay at Cannes. In 2018, after eight years spent teaching and producing films with his younger brother Lee Joong-dong (with projects including July Jung's *A Girl at My Door*), he directed *Burning* featuring American star Steven Yeun. Officially based on a novel by celebrated writer Haruki Murakami, and acclaimed internationally, the film received the FIPRESCI award in Cannes and unsuccessfully ran for the Academy Awards. It received many awards including the Asia Pacific Screen Award, the Munich Film Festival and the Miami Film Festival.

◀ 58

59 ▶

60 ▶

FILMOGRAPHIE

1996 - GREEN FISH (Cho-log-mil-go-gi 초록 물고기)
114 min/35mm/1:85/colour

Synopsis

Mak-dong returns from the army to his family that lives in difficult conditions in a provincial town. At the station, he sees a young woman who is being harrassed by members of the mafia. To find the young woman again, he gets close to the gang's leader who is her lover. .

Production: East Film Company
Screenplay: Lee Chang-dong
Director of photography: Ryoo Young-gil
Editing: Kim Hyun
Music: Lee Dong-joon
Light: Kim Dong-ho
Art director: Joo Byeong-do
Distribution : CJ Entertainment

Cast

Han Seok-kyu *(Mak-dong)*
Shim Hye-jin *(Mi-ae)*
Moon Seung-keun *(Bae Tae-gon)*
Myung Kae-nam *(Kim Yang-gil)*

1999 - PEPPERMINT CANDY (Baghasatang 박하사탕)
129 min/35mm/1:85/colour

Synopsis

In 1999, during a reunion picnic between old friends, Kim Yong-ho commits suicide by walking onto a railway. The film works its way backwards, retracing Yong-ho's story to deliver a portrait of an ordinary man whose life was broken by the conditions created by Korea's contemporary history.

Production : East Film Company
Screenplay: Lee Chang-dong
Director of photography: Kim Hyeong-gu
Editing: Kim Hyun
Music: Lee Jae-jin
Light: Lee Kang-san
Art director: Park Il-hyun
Distribution : CJ Entertainment

Cast

Sol Kyung-gu (*Kim Young-ho*)
Moon So-ri (*Yoon Sun-min*)
Kim Yeo-jin (*Yang Hong-ja*)
Park Se-bum (*Shin Kwang-nam*)
Suh Jung (*Miss Lee*)

2002- OASIS (Oasiseu 오아시스)
132 min/35mm/1:85/colour

Synopsis

A mentally disabled man, Jongdu went to prison instead of his brother, who killed a pedestrian after hitting him with his car. Upon leaving prison, Jongdu visits the victim's family and meets their daughter who has a physical disability. The two marginal fall in love.

Production : East Film Company
Screenplay: Lee Chang-dong
Director of photography: Choi Young-taek
Editing: Kim Hyun
Music: Lee Jae-jin
Light: Choi Youn-taek
Art director: Shin Jum-hee, Oh Sang-man
Distribution : CJ Entertainment

Cast

Sol Kyung-gu (*Hong Jong-du*)
Moon So-ri (*Han Gong-ju*)
Ahn Nae-sang (*Hong Jong-il*)
Choo Kui-jung (*Jong-il's wife*)
Ryoo Seung-wan (*Hong Jong-se*)

2007- SECRET SUNSHINE (Miryang 밀양)
141 min/35mm/2:35/colour

Synopsis

Shin-Ae settles in Miryang, her recently deceased husband's hometown, with her young son Shin-Ae. She pretends to be rich in order to fit into the community. Her child is kidnapped and murdered for money. A lonely mechanic offers to help her, but Shin-Ae fell into religion before recovering her lucidity and rejecting everything.

Production : Pine House Film – Lee Chang-dong
Screenplay: Lee Chang-dong (novel by Lee Cheong-joon)
Executive producer: Lee Han-na
Director of photography: Cho Yong-kyu
Editing: Kim Hyun
Music: Christian Basso
Light: Choo In-shik
Art director: Shin Jum-hee
Distribution : CJ Entertainment

Cast
Jeon Do-yeon (*Lee Shin-ae*)
Song Kang-ho(*Kim Jong-chan*)
Cho Young-jin (*Park Do-sup*)
Kim Young-jae (*Lee Min-ki*)

2010 - POETRY (Si 시)
139 min/35mm/1:85/colour

Synopsis
A poor woman in her sixties, Mija, still works as a home nurse. She is raising her grandson, whose school friend recently committed suicide. Mija, who has a newfound passion for poetry, takes classes with a poet. But she starts suffering from Alzheimer's disease and losing her memory.

Production : Pine House Film, Lee Joon-dong
Screenplay: Lee Chang-dong
Director of photography: Kim Hyun-seok
Assistant réalisateur : Park Jeong-beom
Editing: Kim Hyun
Son : Lee Seung-chul
Light: Kim Ba-da
Art director: Shin Jum-hee
Distribution : N.E.W (Next Entertainment World)

Cast
Yoon Jeong-hee (*Yang Mi-ja*)
Lee David (*Jong-wook*)
Kim Hee-ra (*Kang No-in*)
Ahn Nae-sang (*Père de Kibeom*)
Kim Young-taek (*Kim Young-tak*)

2018 - BURNING (Beo-ning 버닝)
148 min/35mm/1:85/colour

Synopsis
Jong-su, a young introverted deliveryman whose parents are farmers, runs into a former school friend who has become a supermarket entertainer. They start a relationship. Jong-su wants to be a writer, and Haemi wants to be an actress but she suddenly goes on a trip in Africa. When she returns, she brings Ben with her: a mysterious and rich young man who reveals to Jong-su that he likes to burn greenhouses

Production : Pine House Film, Now Film, NHK, Lee Joon-dong, Lee Chang-dong
Screenplay: Oh Jung-mi, Lee Chang-dong (Nouvelle « Barn Burning » by Haruki Murakami)
Executive producer: Ok Gwang-hee
Director of photography: Hong Kyung-pyo (Alex Hong)
Assistant réalisateur: Ha Jeong-su
Editing: Kim Hyun, Kim Da-won
Music: Mowg
Light: Kim Chang-ho
Art director: Shin Jum-hee
Distribution: CGV Arthouse. Well Go USA

Cast
Yoo Ah-in (*Jong-su*)
Steven Yeun (*Ben*)
Jeon Jong-seo (*Haemi*)
Kim Sugyeong (*Hyunju*)
Choi Seungho (*Yongseok*)
Moon Seung-keun

INDEX PHOTO

1 *Poetry*
2 *Burning*
3 *Secret Sunshine*
4 *Green Fish*
5 *Green Fish*
6 *Secret Sunshine*
7 *Secret Sunshine*
8 *Peppermint candy*
9 *Peppermint Candy*
10 *Peppermint Candy ??*
11 *Peppermint Candy*
12 *Green Fish*
13 *Peppermint Candy*
14 *Burning*
15 *Oasis*
16 *Oasis*
17 *Peppermint Candy*
18 *Peppermint Candy*
19 *Burning*
20 *Peppermint Candy*
21 *Peppermint Candy*
22 *Burning*
23 *Secret Sunshine*
24 *Peppermint Candy*
25 *Oasis*
26 *Green Fish*
27 *Peppermint Candy*
28 *Burning*
29 *Burning*
30 *Peppermint Candy*
31 *Burning*

32 *Oasis*
33 *Peppermint Candy*
34 *Burning*
35 *Secret Sunshine*
36 *Poetry*
37 *Burning*
38 *Peppermint*
39 *Peppermint*
40 *Burning*
41 *Peppermint Candy*
42 *Peppermint Candy*
43 *Secret Sunshine*
44 *Oasis*
45 *Oasis*
46 *Peppermint*
47 *Oasis*
48 *Peppermint Candy*
49 *Poetry*
50 *Poetry*
51 *Burning*
52 *Secret Sunshine*
53 *Oasis*
54 *Peppermint*
55 *Peppermint*
56 *Peppermint*
57 *Peppermint*
58 *Burning*
59 *Peppermint*
60 *Peppermint*
61 *Burning*

SERIES 'CINEMA' EDITED BY DANIÈLE RIVIÈRE

In the same series

KIM KI-DUK
Adrien Gombeaud
Anaid Demir
Cedric Lagandré
Catherine Capdeville-Zeng
Danièle Rivière

TSAI MING LIANG
Jean-Pierre Rhem
Olivier Joyard
Danièle Rivière

WONG KAR-WAI
Jean-Marc Lalanne
Ackbar Abbas
David Martinez
Jimmy Ngai

BRUNO DUMONT
Sébastien Ors
Philippe Tancelin
Valérie Jouve

ATOM EGOYAN
Carole Desbarats
Jacinto Lageira
Danièle Rivière
Paul Virilio

PETER GREENAWAY
(*only french version*)
Daniel Caux
Michel Field
Florence de Mèredieu
Philippe Pilard
Michael Nyman

RAOUL RUIZ
(*only french version*)
Christine Buci-Glucksmann
Fabrice Revault D'Allonnes

MANOEL DE OLIVEIRA
(*only french version*)
Yann Lardeau
Philippe Tancelin
Jacques Parsi